The Flirtologist's Guide To Dating
Where To Go And What To Say
To Date And Feel Great!

by Jill Spiegel
with Joe Brozic

The Flirtologist's Guide To Dating

ISBN 0-9643325-9-0
Published by Joe Brozic through Goal Getters.

Goal Getters
3943 Chowen Ave. S.
Minneapolis, MN 55410
phone: 612-925-5814 fax: 612-922-8241 website:
www.Flirtnow.com

Printed in The United States of America
Printed by Park Printing, Minneapolis, Minnesota
Written- Jill Spiegel
Proofread- Kris Dunlap
Edited and Published- Joe Brozic

Jill Spiegel is also the author of Flirting For Success, Flirting With Spirituality and The Pocket Pep Talk.

To contact Jill for appearances or to order her books and tapes, contact Goal Getters: 612-925-5814 or email her: Jill@Flirtnow.com

Jill Spiegel is a Flirtologist/Author/Speaker. Her website is www.Flirtnow.com

Table of Contents

What Every Dater Needs To Know!
Dating Do's and Don'ts........................**93**

Turn Moments Into Magic!
Celebrate Your Life Every Day.....150

READY, SET, DATE!
WHAT TO SAY

YOUR PERSONAL FLIRTOLOGIST

Hi! It's me Jill Spiegel, The Flirtologist. I'm thrilled to meet you! I think it's so cool that you are reading this book. You are a positive thinker. I love that!

Now, before we go any further, you may be wondering, what is a Flirtologist? I share the art of flirting with the magic in people and life by connecting in a warm, genuine and playful way. When you flirt like that, your world opens up. You meet people you "click with" everywhere. You feel magically guided by life. You create supportive relationships. You date and feel great! Sound good? Well, there's more. I'll be right there with you every step of the way as YOUR own personal Flirtologist! You've seen me on *The Oprah Winfrey Show* and *The Today Show* where, through a walkie-talkie, I coach and encourage daters, inspiring them for dating confidence and success.

This guide book is just like having me whisper in your ear, cheering you on! I give you mini-scripts, effective things to say in specific scenarios and how to develop a mindset that makes you attract what you desire. Plus, I'll answer the most asked questions I've received over the years about dating in our modern world.

Now, if you have found dating challenging you are

not alone. For over a decade, I've been giving relationship seminars and coaching people on dating. Not once have I heard someone say, "Dating is easy." At times dating is challenging, nerve-wracking and confusing. It's also exciting, rewarding and exhilarating! I can understand the perils of dating. I've had my own roller coaster ride through the romance arena. The first talk show I appeared on, the subject was women who date jerks-and I was the expert! Looking back, I feel grateful I went through every experience. I learned to work on my self-esteem and attract healthy people into my life.

All of our dating struggles happen for a reason. They lead us into finding ourselves and creating fulfilling relationships. I am certain that anyone who approaches life positively, like you, and hopes for a healthy, romantic companionship finds it! The strategies in this guide work for my dating students and they will work for you, too. You are right on track for dating success. It's time to date and feel great!

We're off to a great start!

BE IN *THE NOTICE ZONE*

There is one vast and exciting dating service that's open seven days a week: Life! Whenever you leave your home and go anywhere, you encounter people. You can meet people you click with anytime, everywhere by being alert and in the moment. The universe works magically! People you are meant to meet are all around you.

Remember the show Starsky and Hutch from the '70s? I had such a crush on Starsky! He was played by actor Paul Michael Glazer, who met his wife, Elizabeth, at a traffic stop. They were each driving down the road in their cars when they both came to a stoplight. They looked over at each other, smiled and felt a connection, an energy. "Starsky" said "Pull over. Let's talk." In *The Notice Zone*, even a stoplight has magic!

When you are in *The Notice Zone* you are alert and open to making connections. One thing that stops us from being alert is being buried in thought as we walk about our day. We may be going over our schedules or worrying about something we said yesterday. When we do that we stare at the ground, missing all the faces around us. In a sense we make ourselves invisible.

Be in *The Notice Zone*. Make a commitment to yourself to be in the moment whenever you are around people. Hold your head up, look around. Notice every-thing and everyone. You'll be amazed at how many people and things catch your eye! Once you are in *The Notice Zone,* start smiling at people and practice being friendly. Say hi to new faces as if you've known them forever. Men always tell me they only feel comfortable approaching a woman when she's smiling. Most people feel the same way. When you reach out in a friendly way, you get a positive response.

(Now you may be thinking, what if you don't get a positive response? We'll get to that soon when we do *Rock 'N' Roll Rejection*, I promise! Right now let's get back to *The Notice Zone*.)

I once coached a female artist who crossed paths with a businessman while riding in the same elevator on their way to work. The first few months they said nothing. During their third month of silence she came to my seminar. I coached her to reach out. By the fourth month they were talking. By the fifth month, he asked her out. One year later they married. Millions of couples and happy daters have met in everyday places by being alert and receptive. It can happen to you, too!

YOUR SCRIPT

Remember: The universe strategically places you next to and near people you are supposed to meet. Be in *The Notice Zone*: Be alert around people. Be friendly. Talk to new faces as if you've known them

forever. **Say your name and they'll tell you theirs. Exchanging names heightens a connection.**

Use this line: *Hi!*

Do *The Name Exchange*:

My name is _____. What's yours?

   Awesome! You have the idea. You are in *The Notice Zone*! Now let's talk about some more ways to reach out and start conversations. There are four easy, effective and natural ways to connect with people everywhere.

I call them:

THE FABULOUS FOUR CONNEC- TORS

1. THE POSITIVE COMMENT CUE

2. THE CARING COMPLIMENT CATCH

3. THE ASK A QUESTION INVITATION

4. THE HONEST, DIRECT LINE CHARM

Now, anyone can use these connectors to reach out. We are in the modern dating world where women can start conversations with men. Men can start conversations with women. Women can reach out to women and men can reach out to men. People can be friendly to people! The more you extend yourself to others, the more you open up your world.

You are about to master *The Fabulous Four Connectors*!

THE POSITIVE COMMENT CUE

Want to make someone's day? Say something positive. The moment you say something positive to someone, you boost their spirit and draw them to you. You also feel a sense of exhilaration! Surveys on first impressions show that making positive comments to people has an uplifting psychological effect on their mood.

When you're flirting for romance, you don't have to be seductive or witty. The top three qualities people look for when meeting someone are genuineness, kindness and empathy. So forget that clever line. Even simple comments about the weather make people feel good. Think about it. Imagine you were riding in an elevator and a new face walked in and said "Isn't it a beautiful day?" Would you think that statement wasn't clever enough to respond to?

Look back at your life and think about your relationships and friendships. How did they begin? Do you remember the first words that were said? Were they brilliant - or common, warm and friendly?

The first time Paul McCartney met his wife Linda was at a busy nightclub. He spotted her and wanted to meet her. As she walked past his table, he stood up and cleared his throat. He said, "Hello. My name is Paul." A simple introduction that led to an incredible 30-year romance!

One guy who attended my dating seminar told me, "I get nervous with women, but I know I can be a positive person so I'll give *The Positive Comment Cue* a try." A week later, he told me what happened. "I walked into this bagel shop and noticed this cute gal in front of me in line. I said to her 'Fresh bagels! They smell good.' She agreed, and we had a conversation about food. I made a mental note to go to the same bagel shop the next day at the same time and there she was. I said to her, 'They still smell good!' I could have kicked myself. That was the same thing I said yesterday, but she smiled and talked to me anyway. We're going out Saturday night!"

YOUR SCRIPT

No matter where you are, you can always think of something positive to say.

Some positive comments to try out are:

Perfect weather today!

I love this store! (park) (restaurant)

Getting in gear for Monday!

I'm psyched it's Friday! (Wednesday, Thursday)

The food is great here!

What a beautiful park!

This part of town is my favorite area!

Looks like the sun is coming out!

Great day for a walk!

Choose a line you connect with and the conversation flows naturally.

Love it! Now on to your next connector.

THE CARING COMPLIMENT CATCH

Once I was about to go on a local talk show and a local politician was on after me. I was looking in the mirror fixing my hair when he whispered to me, "Looking good." I thought, Who is that? I like him. I'm voting for him!

Everybody craves compliments and positive feedback. When you sincerely do that for someone you make their day and they feel good about you immediately. I had the chance to compliment one of my heroes, Mary Tyler Moore, when she came to town to make a speech. During the part for audience questions I raised my hand. She called on me! My lips started quivering with excitement and I said, "Mary, you are such a great actress, an awesome writer, a terrific dancer, and a wonderful speaker! Out of everything in your career what do you like doing the most?" My lips were still quivering when she looked me straight in the eye, quivered her lips and said with a big smile, "Listening to you!"

Start right now. Start paying compliments to people you encounter throughout the day. The more compliments you give, the more you open your life and the better you feel. Compliments are gifts which ripple out like waves and flow back to you. You actually feel the power of the vibrations you're sending out! Plus, creating and spreading goodness builds a positive energy around you, which people pick up on.

Also make sure you say "thank you" to all the compliments that come back to you. Think of compliments as gifts and accept them with warmth and appreciation.

YOUR SCRIPT

One of the most effective openers is reaching out with a compliment:

I love your jacket! or *What a cool tie!* or *You have a great smile.* **You could start with a positive comment and then you can ease your way into complimenting people directly:**

I love Fridays. Hey, what a sharp suit!

Another powerful compliment is: *You look like (a certain celebrity,)* or *You remind me of (a certain celebrity.)* **Someone once said to me, "You look like Sandra Bullock." I love Sandra! I was so flattered! I once told a bank teller, "You remind me of Denzel Washington. I bet tons of people have told you that." He smiled and said, "A few people have. It feels good every time!"**

Accepting compliments is also critical. By accepting a compliment you wear it and you share it with the person who gave you the compliment. If accepting compliments is difficult for you at first, it will be easier for you if you give a compliment while you accept one. That way you share the "spotlight." Say: *Thank you. You made my day.* **or**

Thanks. That makes me feel so good! or *Wow! What a nice thing to say! Thank you!*

Two connectors down. Two more to go!

THE ASK A QUESTION INVITATION

I was on an airplane once reading a book called *How To Have An Out-Of-Body Experience*. I'm fascinated by supernatural subjects, but I was hiding the book from the guy seated next to me. He looked like a serious businessman, and I thought my book might seem off-putting to him. All of a sudden I heard, "Good book?" I was so excited he reached out that I blurted, "It's about how to have an out-of-body experience, ever have one?" Did I just ask him that? I started to shrink when he smiled and said, "Actually I have. It was at work last year. My name is Keith, by the way. Let me tell you what happened..." We talked the whole flight! Asking a question shows us we have something in common with everybody.

Asking a question also immediately engages people and makes them feel helpful and needed. So try this method wherever you go and see how magic happens. Using a walkie-talkie on Britain's *This Morning Show*, I coached a girl from Manchester who wore a hidden ear piece. She was in London for the day. As she walked down the street in a quaint area, I watched her on a hidden camera from a van nearby. I whispered simple questions she could say to the other Londoners like, "Excuse me. I'm new to this area. Do you know a good restaurant here?" or "Hi. I need a little help. I'm in for the day from Manchester. Do you know if there's a coffee shop around here?" These simple questions led to longer flirtations and soon she had a lunch date with a local London guy!

YOUR SCRIPT

When you reach out and ask questions, your life blooms with coincidences, and you find you have something in common with everybody. Next time you walk down the street, stop someone and say:

Excuse me, do you know a good place to eat around here? **or**

Hi! Do know what time it is? **or**

Hello! I wonder if you could point me in the direction of _____ street? **or**

Pardon me. I love your jacket! Did you get that here in town?

Great! Once you've asked that question, keep the conversation going by following up with a little information about yourself and then ask another question:

Excuse me, Do you know a good place to eat around here? I'm new to the area and I need a recommendation. A good meal always puts me in a good mood. What's your favorite place?

Hi! Do know what time it is? Thanks! I left my watch

at home. Oh, I like your watch. Did you get that here?

Hello! I wonder if you could point me in the direction of _____ street? I thought I knew where I was going, but I got lost. I need a compass! Do you know the area well?

THE HONEST, DIRECT LINE CHARM

"Your legs must be tired because they've been running through my mind all night." During one of my appearances on an *Oprah* show called "Eavesdropping On Pickup Lines," one guy told us he uses that line. You could just hear the audience cringe over lines like that. Nobody wants to be approached by someone who is phony or overly corny.

Now sometimes a corny line can be flattering if said with a genuine sense of humor. While working on a flirting story for the news, I was sitting with an attractive female reporter at a bar. A man approached her and gently said, "What do you do all day besides look beautiful?" He was so sweet and non-threatening, even I blushed. I don't recommend that line to everyone. It depends if you are comfortable with it. Most people are nervous when they approach someone else and saying a line like that seems too forward. So before I give you *The Honest, Direct Line Charm*, let's talk about nerves.

One of the comments I hear from daters is "I want to break the ice, but I get so nervous!" Here's some exciting news: Nervousness is good! Being nervous is charming when you reach out and flirt. It shows that you care and a little vulnerability is appealing. So use it to your advantage. Own it!

During one seminar I coached a guy, who felt a little nervous, to use *The Honest, Direct Line Charm* on a woman he had his eye on for awhile. After he said it, she told him. "Gosh. I'm in a relationship, but you are so sweet. Why don't you give me your number anyway. I know a few single girls who would like you."

YOUR SCRIPT

Hold your head up, smile and say *The Honest, Direct Line Charm*:

Excuse me, my name is _____. I'm a little nervous right now,

but when I saw you I knew if I didn't introduce myself tonight,

I'd really regret it tomorrow.

or

Hi! I'm _____. I have to confess. I'm a bit nervous to break the ice with you, but when I saw you I knew if I didn't say something now, I'd be upset with myself tomorrow!

Way to go! You've mastered *The Fabulous Four Connectors*! Now that you've reached out, let's get into the conversation and the vital next step: *The Commitment Check.*

THE COMMITMENT CHECK for women to men

Men and Wedding Rings

"I was so shocked," a dater once said to me. "I had been chatting with this guy for 15 minutes, and I was sure we were hitting it off. I did *The Name Exchange*, and I asked him out for coffee. He told me his wife would probably mind. Wife?! He wasn't even wearing a ring. How can you even tell if someone is married?"

Many women tell me that they meet nice men who don't wear their wedding rings, which is confusing in the dating world. It's important to remember that even though a man isn't wearing a ring, it doesn't automatically mean he's looking to date outside his marriage. Many men dislike wearing jewelry or have a job which makes wearing jewelry difficult.

So if you're interested in someone, it's always helpful to learn up front if they're available. Do that by asking him a question involving his "possible" family.

For example, if you first meet at a public place like a grocery or clothing store, you could say, "Do you and your wife shop here a lot?" If you meet at a party, you could say, "Did your wife or family come with you tonight?"

<u>YOUR SCRIPT</u>

When you meet a guy for the first time, find out within the first five minutes if he's married by doing *The Commitment Check*. Say to him:

Do you and your wife come here a lot?

or

Do you and your family live nearby?

or *Is your family here with you today?*

You've got it! Great for the gals.

Now for men.....

THE COMMITMENT CHECK for men to women

Women and wedding rings

"What a beautiful ring," a guy once said to me when we were waiting in line at a drugstore. We had been chatting for a bit, when he pointed to my engagement ring, a ruby, and asked me about it. It wasn't until I left the store when I realized, he's doing *The Commitment Check!*

Women sometimes complain that married men don't wear their wedding rings, while men complain that single women confuse them by wearing too many rings, even on their wedding finger. One guy in class told us, "The problem is women wear rings on their wedding finger and sometimes it doesn't look like a wedding ring, but it's hard to tell!" So compliment her on her wedding ring or drop an early hint to find out her status. One thing you could say is "Does your husband come here with you, too?"

YOUR SCRIPT

When she's wearing an unusual ring on her wedding finger, find out if she's married by pointing to the ring and pay her a compliment:

What an unusual wedding ring. I really like that.

If she's married, she'll say "Thank you" and proba-

bly explain why she chose that ring. If she's single and not interested, she'll probably just say "Thanks." And if she's single and interested, she'll say, "Oh thanks, but I'm not married."

Some daters who are divorced tell me they feel awkward saying "I'm divorced" right up front. They see themselves as single. If you are divorced and you meet a new face who asks about your relationship status, you can say you are divorced or you can say you are single or newly single or re-available. If you say newly single and they ask if you have kids, then you can let them know about your previous marriage: *Yes, I have three kids. I was married eight years.*

Even when someone does wear a wedding ring, they could be a widow or widower. Find out their status in the beginning of meeting them: *Did your family (husband) come here with you today?*

Super job on *The Commitment Check*! Let's keep going. When we are talking to or flirting with someone for the first time, the question usually comes up: "What do you do?" Let's take a look at that common question, and I'll tell you the most powerful and exciting way to respond!

THE "WHAT DO YOU DO?" RESPONSE

The American/European Flirting Introduction

"What do you do?" In America we interpret that question as "What do you do for work?" In Europe people interpret that question as "What do you do for fun?" The most powerful response to this question is to combine the American and European methods by describing both your job and your hobbies with a sense of passion and purpose.

In my seminars we practice explaining our jobs in a way that other people can feel our pride and connect with our occupation. For example, one guy in class said when he tells people he is an electrician, their eyes glaze over. That's because some people may not know a lot about his particular occupation and need more explanation. He found a way to engage people by changing his answer to, "You know when you walk in the house and turn the lights on, check your answering machine, use your remote control? That is my expertise. I'm an electrician, and I do all the wiring behind the scenes. I really enjoy it." See how that answer draws people in and helps them relate to his work?

Always describe your life positively. If you are currently not working at a paying job or are in between jobs, tell people, "I'm a student of life," or "I'm in discovery! I've always wanted to learn guitar and now I'm getting my chance!" When I visited Liverpool,

England, with my sister, two guys gave us a ride back to the train station. The guy in the passenger seat had a cast around his arm. I said to them, "What do you guys do?" The guy with the cast held up his arm and said joyously, "I'm not working!" He was charming!

After you've described your work in a purposeful, relatable way, make sure you mention your hobby. You never know where you may find common interests with someone else. Also, by mentioning your hobby you inspire people! You role model valuing interests beyond your job and having balance in life. Describe your hobby in the same way as you do your job, with passion and purpose. "When I'm not working at my job, I enjoy nature walks. I love bird watching!"

YOUR TURN

Take a moment and think about your life. How can you describe your job in a way that anyone could relate to it? If you are not working a paying job, what are you passionate about? What are your hobbies? What excites you about them?

YOUR SCRIPT

Try it: *I work at _____, and I enjoy helping people _____. I also like to (listen to or watch or read or play) _____. I'm such a fan of _____.*

MORE EXAMPLES OF *THE "WHAT DO YOU DO" RESPONSE*

When people ask you what you do, inspire them by describing both your job and your hobbies with passion and purpose.

Example: Day-care worker who likes sports.

Response: *I'm in early child development. I find it so meaningful to encourage children and help shape their self-esteem. I also love to play basketball. How about you?*

Example: Government debt collector who likes cooking.

Response: *I help keep the finances in the state balanced. I work at the County Collection agency, and I help people with their records. I like empathizing with people and putting them at ease. I also love to cook, especially Italian food. How about you?*

Example: Medical supply salesperson who likes music.

Response: *I sell medical supplies, including equipment that rehabilitates people with injuries, which I find so rewarding. My hobby is music. Right now I'm into the Elvis remix.*

If you are unemployed try: *Right now I'm enjoying*

my freedom from the working world. I've been exploring my passion in photography and hiking, and I'm having a blast. What are your hobbies? or *I work as a volunteer. I also hike a lot for fun. I love being a student of life! What do you love to do?*

Using these ideas, create your new American/European Introduction!

Awesome! You have *The American/European Flirting Introduction* down. Now let's get from that first conversation to the first date or pre-date.

FROM THE FIRST CONVERSATION TO THE PRE-DATE

You spot him (or her). You reach out. You feel the "clickage." How do you go from the first conversation to the first date? You can ask for a date right there by saying, "Would you like to go out next Friday night?" You could also take things a little slower, which I recommend. You are still getting to know this person and you might want some more talking time before setting up a longer evening date.

Set up a pre-date, a casual way to spend more time with him or her. For the next get-together, suggest grabbing a coffee or taking a walk, activities that give you time to talk but don't have to take a lot of time. Sometimes you can set up a pre-date right on the spot.

Once I coached a sweet guy who was shopping at a grocery store. While pushing his cart down the aisles, he spotted a warm female face. I whispered to him to say, "Hi! You look like you know what you are doing, and I'm a little lost. Can you show me where the hair care products are?" She was so receptive, that after they chatted a bit, I decided to have him suggest the pre-date, "Thanks so much for your help. Hey, there's a coffee shop right in this store. I have 20 minutes. You want to grab a cup?" She said yes!

Always have your business card or a paper and pen with you so you're ready to give your phone number. One guy in my dating seminar made his own personal card describing his personality traits. He has his name printed and below his name it says whimsical, laid-back, good communicator. Once you've given your number don't sit by the phone. Let go.

Let life's special timing work. Continue to reach out and keep flirting with yourself.

YOUR SCRIPT

Suggesting coffee or a walk eases you two into the "getting to know you" phase, as these activities can

be half an hour to one hour whereas a date is longer. By giving your number, you don't have to ask for one. You can give your work or home number or email address depending on what makes you feel more comfortable.

Remember this approach when you want to take a conversation to the pre-date:

I have had so much talking to you, and now I have to run. Would you like to go out for coffee or a walk sometime and talk some more? Here's my card (or home number). Call me if you're interested. Tuesday nights are good to reach me. **By mentioning a good time to reach you, you show you have a full life while at the same time hinting interest.**

To set up coffee at the first meeting, say: *Hey, there's a coffee shop right next door. I have about half an hour before I have to be somewhere. Would you like to join me?*

A+! Let's review:

Step 1: Be in *The Notice Zone*
Step 2: Do one of *The Fabulous Four Connectors*

Step 3: Do *The Commitment Check*

Step 4: *The "What do you do?" Response*

Step 5: From *The Conversation To The Pre-Date* Approach

Remember to do *The Name Exchange* at some point.

You can say: *My name is _____. What's yours?*

or *I'm _____, and you are?*

If you are in the middle of a sentence, you can interject,

My name is _____, by the way, and you?

You are on a roll. Let's keep going!

THE FLIRT WITH YOURSELF MINDSET

Before you talk to anyone, it's so important to listen to the way you talk to yourself. So many people hold themselves back from reaching out or flirting. They psyche themselves out, thinking they have to be witty or seductive, which is a total misconception. Remember flirting is about making friends. All good relationships, platonic and romantic, are grounded in friendship and mutual respect, so start there. Think friendly. The other reason people don't reach out to others or flirt is because they think they can't. They fill themselves with fear by thinking, what are they going to think of me or what if they don't think like me? We fall into a trap of self-judgement. Here's a magic solution: What you tell yourself, you become and attract. So start flirting with yourself right now and life flirts back with you. Think: I am fun, I am caring, I am a catch! Compliment yourself and focus on your gifts. By repeating these personal flirtations you live them! We create ourselves every day by the way we think.

My own self-esteem used to be low. I lived in a state of constant insecurity and negative self-talk. After practicing personal flirtations, my life changed. One of my favorite flirtations is "I am a Beatle." I love their spirit! One day I was whispering my Beatle flirtation when I walked by a small boy who said, "Look-it's a Beatle!" I was startled! Then I noticed he was looking at a beetle insect. The synchronicity was awesome! Life was flirting back with me. I kept saying "I am a

Beatle." Then the top morning show in London called me to make an appearance! I went to London wearing a '60s styled black and white striped outfit, and I hailed a cab. I told the driver I came to Christen myself a Beatle. He said, "I'll take you to Abbey Road where The Beatles walked, and I'll be your photographer." It's so cool how people root for you when you share your dreams. When we arrived at Abbey Road he said, "Now march forward," and snapped a picture.

Once the picture was developed, I was thrilled to see my black and white outfit matches the stripes on the lamppost and the street! More synchronicity! To me, the black and white symbolizes the duality in life. Life is pain and joy. Sometimes we need to go through the rough times to appreciate and create more joyous experiences. To think I had been in London in college and was miserable with my negative self-talk. Now years later, I was back in London feeling like a Beatle! My personal flirtations worked! I continue to work on my self-esteem. In fact, I'm working on my self-esteem right now. I promise you that if you make it a habit to flirt with yourself every day, you will radiate a contagious energy. People will be drawn to you and your life will be filled with joy and magic!

THE FLIRT WITH YOURSELF MINDSET script

YOUR TURN

Every morning when you look in the mirror and throughout the day, flirt with yourself. Declare *I am!* **Even saying I will be or I'm trying to be holds your dream at a distance. You must say** *I am.* **Think or say out loud:** *I am confident* **or** *I am loving and appealing* **or** *I am drawing positive people and loving relationships into my life* **or** *I trust myself* **or** *I rock!* **You can make up your own flirtation. Whatever you aspire to be, tell yourself you are and the universe flirts back with you! Remember, what you tell yourself, you become.**

YOUR SCRIPT

TRANSFORMING NEGATIVE THOUGHTS TO POSITIVE FLIRTATIOUS WHISPERS

egative Thoughts	Positive Flirtatious Whispers
u interpret your dating experiences : **I am unlucky in love.**	Tell yourself this: **Life is preparing me for healthy relationships.**

egative Thoughts	Positive Flirtatious Whispers
meone role modeled to you: **m not good enough unless I'm a relationship.**	Repeat to yourself this: **I am lovable and special on my own.**

Negative Thoughts	Positive Flirtatious Whispers
You were told often and believe:	Live by the truth:
I am not good enough.	**I am equal to everyone and special in my own way.**

Negative Thoughts	Positive Flirtatious Whispers
You have formed the habit of thinking:	Practice thinking this and believe:
I would rather settle than be alone.	**I am great on my own, and hold out for the right perso**

Negative Thoughts	Positive Flirtatious Whispers
You have been taught to compare yourself to others and tell yourself:	Replace those thoughts with:
She (he) has so much more going for her (him) than I do.	**My journey and special gif are unique and meant for r**

Practice Positive Flirtatious Whispers Every Day.

Watch Your Life Transform.

Flirt with yourself now!

Great job! You excel at understanding flirting and reaching out! Once you start practicing these techniques, you are more confident each time. Now, let's move on to some dating myths. You'll just love the truth about dating!

MYTH: AN ATTRACTIVE APPEARANCE IS THE KEY TO FLIRTING.

TRUTH: PEOPLE RESPOND TO EACH OTHER'S ESSENCES.

THE ESSENCE FACTOR

I once received an email from a woman who felt confused about this very issue. She wrote, "I'm in my mid 20s and I would love to find a boyfriend. Last weekend I went to a party with my girlfriends, and there was a guy there who was so gorgeous. He looked like Brad Pitt. He asked me to dance. Me?!! We danced and talked most of the night and at the end of the night he wanted to kiss me and go out. The problem is I just couldn't. I didn't feel the urge to kiss him. I wasn't even excited to have a date with him. There was something missing for me. My friends couldn't believe I passed on Brad Pitt's twin! Is something wrong with me?" I assured her that there was nothing wrong with her and emailed her that if it doesn't feel right, don't do it.

Just because someone looks "good" doesn't mean we'll be attracted to them. Attraction, feeling drawn to and excited by each other, involves so much more than just enjoying someone's outward appearance. It's also about feeling that you two "click," that your personalities mesh and you are bonding on an emotional level. People respond to each other's essences; who we are inside. Always listen to your heart! Let your intuition tell you when you have a natural chemistry with someone.

One woman wrote to me, "I am dating a wonderful man who happens to be disabled. His essence is so powerful, kind and brave. I feel like the luckiest woman in the world." Here's another email from one of my dating students. He wrote, "I met the most wonderful woman. She's smart, sweet, loving, and we have so much in common. She's 12 years older than me, but it's not an issue. It's like you say in class, our 'essences' are what matters. She and I are the perfect fit."

YOUR TURN

Essences are what we project from the inside out, such as playful, mysterious, friendly, down-to-earth, kind, strong, calm, energetic, healing, soft, tough, mature, honest, childlike and so much more. People can have several qualities that make up their

essence.

Think of the people you are drawn to.

How would you describe their essence?

How would you describe your essence?

I like your essence. Now on to our next technique!

MYTH: REJECTION IS AWFUL.

TRUTH: REJECTION IS A GIFT.

ROCK 'N' ROLL REJECTION

In the world of dating, everyone is special and unique. No one is better or greater than anyone else, just different. The problem we often fall into is thinking that something is wrong with us if another person doesn't return our interest or breaks up with us. Don't let your self-esteem depend on someone's response. Here's the good news: rejection is a favor. It's the universe saying to us, "It's time to move on. This person is not (or no longer) the right fit for you at this time." Dating is like clothes shopping. You need to try on several outfits to see which one is right for you. Sometimes an outfit looks great on us for awhile, but eventually we may outgrow it.

When it comes to rejection, think of yourself as a rock star. Rock stars know they are talented and they believe in themselves. The Beatles were rejected by the first record label they approached. They were told, "Guitar groups are on their way out." Did that stop The Beatles? No way! John Lennon said, "We're already the best band in the world. It's just a matter of the world finding out." Now that's what I call *Rock 'N' Roll Rejection*! There is a popular singer named Everlast. I saw him on a television interview. The interviewer asked him how he deals with people who criticize him or don't like his music. Everlast explained his philosophy: "It doesn't bother me. It's like I say at the end of every concert, 'If you didn't get it, it wasn't for you.'" You too can have a rock 'n' roll attitude about rejection. Know you are powerful and appealing! If someone doesn't respond to your charm, tell yourself, "If they don't get me, they're not right for me."

I remember a time in my life when I was desperate for this one guy to like me as much as I liked him. When I was around him I tried so hard to be engaging. He knew I was "into" him, but he didn't feel the same way. I was crushed. Soon I developed an inferiority complex, constantly telling myself I don't measure up for him. I begged the universe, "Please let him like me! Please let it work out!" The universe knew what was best for me and it didn't work out. Over time, I realized his rejection of me had nothing to do with me being "not good enough" or undesirable or unlovable. It just wasn't a fit. When I look at my life now I can't even imagine being with that guy today! Everything turns out the way it's meant to.

YOUR TURN

If someone doesn't return your call or affection, say to life:

Thank you for the favor. I'm moving on with my life knowing I'm lovable and desirable, and I'm drawing the right person to me. **Remind yourself every day that you are special and equal to everyone in the universe. Have a** *Rock 'N' Roll Rejection* **outlook:**

If they didn't feel romantic about me, they weren't the right person for me.

MYTH: ALL THE GOOD ONES ARE TAKEN.

TRUTH: THERE ARE 100 MILLION SIN-GLES IN THE UNITED STATES.

THE ABUNDANT DATING PHILOSOPHY

Sometimes meeting other singles seems harder as we grow older. That's because when you're younger, there are single, eligible people everywhere. Remember in college when you would break up with someone? Then you would walk into your math lecture and sit next to a new appealing single. Dating was in the air everywhere and single people were everywhere, too.

When you're older you may spend most of your time at one job. You see the same small group of people every day. So it seems like the "dating pool" is smaller. A recent survey said there are 100 million singles in the United States. There are enough singles for everyone to date and find companionship. Take classes, learn hobbies, become socially involved in your community, and be alert to the people around you wherever you go. Open up your world. You have already opened up your life by reading this book! All you need to do is continue to make this kind of effort to meet more people and you'll feel the abundance again.

Another reason dating feels tougher as you get older is you realize what truly matters to you in a partner. You may exclude yourself from dating certain people who you may have dated when you were younger and developing a long term future wasn't your concern. As one gal in class told us, "I recently met this fun, free-spirited bohemian guy who I would have dated for sure in my 20s. Now that I'm in my 40s, I want to settle down with someone and this guy never stays in one place or has any financial resources. He's sweet, but not what I'm looking for in a lifetime companion." Knowing what you want is healthy. Don't settle for less!

YOUR TURN

When you think the dating pool is small, remind yourself:

There are 100 million singles in the United States.

The right person for me is out there and I am drawing him/her to me.

Live your life with an attitude of abundance. There is
always enough for everyone. You rock!

MYTH: FINDING DATES IS ABOUT HARD WORK AND EFFORT.

TRUTH: FINDING DATES CAN HAPPEN NATURALLY.

THE NON-DATING METHOD

The non-dater. It's the method the down-to-earth
actress Sandra Bullock uses. I saw Sandra on a television interview and a reporter asked her if she was dating
anybody. Sandra said, "I don't date. I think it's awkward and uncomfortable. I just live my life and make
friends and if a friendship turns into romance, great!"
The first time I mentioned that in my dating class, a
distinguished man raised his hand and said, "Yes. I
think I am going to subscribe to The Sandra Bullock
Non-Dating Method." You can, too! You don't have to
consider yourself a dater. You can still believe in and
expect romance in your life without actively or con-
sciously dating. Live your life and be open to developing acquaintances everywhere. One guy told me, "I
never had time to date. I was so busy with work, traveling and going to meetings. Then the strangest thing
happened. I had to catch this one train, and I missed it

three times! That never happens to me. Finally, I made the fourth train. I started telling the woman seated next to me about my missed train troubles. She was so understanding. Today she is my wife!" Another woman married her soulmate because of a mailman's "mistake." The mailman delivered her letter to a man who lived down the street. When the man received the letter, he brought it to her personally and love blossomed. They even invited the mailman to their wedding!

Life is filled with magical surprises. By living your life and believing in magic you meet new people all the time. So if you ever feel like you should be trying harder at finding dates, tell yourself for now you are doing *The Non-Dating Method* and then expect to meet interesting people wherever you go. In no time, you will feel hopeful and proud of yourself for subscribing to life's natural dating service. You see that life has a miraculous way of bringing special people into our path all the time!

YOUR SCRIPT

Once you get into a conversation with someone, you could casually say:

I have half an hour before my next appointment. Would you like to grab a coffee?

or *I'm going to the parade later. Want to join me?* **or** *There's a great free outdoor concert (art opening) tonight. Want to meet me there?*

SUMMARY PEP TALK

GREAT JOB! You finished your first chapter and you are doing amazing! Now, I know that was a lot to soak in. Just remember the more you practice the tips you learned, the easier it gets until all your new skills are a habit! Let's review some ideas:

*Life is your 24-hour dating service with 100 million singles in the U.S. alone. The universe puts you next to people you are meant to meet. You can meet people anywhere and everywhere. Practice *Positive Flirtatious Whispers* every day. Make your self-esteem your hobby. Remember, all flirting starts with being friendly!

*Remember our steps. Step 1: Be in *The Notice Zone*. Step 2: Do one of *The Fabulous Four Connectors*. Step 3: Do *The Commitment Check*. Step 4: *The "What do you do?" Response*. Step 5: From *The Conversation To The Pre-Date* Approach. Add *The Name Exchange* during one of these steps.

*Rejection is a gift—or life telling you this person is not right for you. Be a rock 'n' roller about rejection! Finding dates can happen naturally, so you can always consider yourself a non-dater. Live your life, make friends and see what develops from there!

YOUR 24-HOUR DATING
SERVICE!
WHERE TO GO

You aced the last chapter. Way to go! Now on to where to go to meet people. In my dating classes, I have people make a list of all the places they frequent just by living their everyday lives. Guess what? There is an awesome dating strategy for every common place we visit!

Meeting people in grocery stores with
The Grocery Store Catch.

Meeting people in clothing stores with
The Clothing Store Connection.

Meeting people at parks with
The Park Pick-Me-Up.

Meeting people at the gym with
The Gym Gem.

Meeting people at work with
The Firm Find.

Meeting people at sporting activities with
The Sports Spot.

Meeting people at parties with
The Party Place.

Meeting people at bars with
The Bar Star.

Meeting people at coffee shops with
The Coffee Shop Stop.

Meeting people with
The Cleaners Corner and The Laundromat Match.

Meeting people at Churches or Temples with
The Worship Watch.

Meeting people at your apartment complex or in your
neighborhood with
The Home Zone.

Meeting people at salons with
The Hair Cut Setup.

Meeting people through taking a class with
The Classes Masses.

Meeting people at bookstores through
The Bookstore Bet.

Meeting people through volunteering with
The Volunteer Victory.

Meeting people by walking around with
The Street Greet, Celebrity Style.

Meeting people through other cool people you know
through
The Inner Circle Sanction.

Meeting people in line with
The Line Find.

  Great! Now let's take a closer look at each of these
strategies. As you read each section, think about your
own life. Can you see yourself connecting with people
at these various places?

  Me, too!

THE GROCERY STORE CATCH

  She sees a cute guy in the orange juice section! On
one of my *Oprah* appearances, I coached a girl at her
local grocery store. When she spotted that cute guy, I
whispered to her to say, "There are so many brands.
What do you buy?" Soon they were talking and before
you know it, they exchanged phone numbers. Oprah
turned and said "Meeting in the orange section!" It can
happen to you, too! Grocery stores are one of the top-
rated places for meeting people. They have all the ele-

ments that make connecting with others easy. Eligible singles are passing through at all hours. The environment is relaxed. You have something in common with everyone-shopping and food.

Next time you go to a grocery store, practice being friendly and connect. Say hi warmly and smile! Notice the other people shopping there. What can you learn about them by glancing in their cart? One of my past dating students met a guy while shopping at a co-op. She glanced in his cart behind her in the check out line, and she said to him, "I think I see a fellow vegetarian."

Now here is Plan B, in case you spot that cutie and you feel tongue-tied. Lightly bump his/her cart and say, "Whoops! I guess I'm a bad driver today." You've gotten his/her attention and you did it with humor. Remember you also can always reach out by paying a compliment or asking a question. "Excuse me, do you know where the dairy section is?" could be the opening that leads you to your soulmate...you never know!

YOUR SCRIPT

Step 1. Ask a clerk at your grocery store when the busiest hours are for singles. If that's not your style, experiment yourself by going shopping at different times and seeing who shops during those hours.

Step 2. Warm-up for this technique by going to the

grocery store and just saying hi to people. Soon you'll feel ready to start conversations.

Step 3. Start conversations. In the grocery store you can say to someone:

Excuse me. Do you know where the bread section is? I've never shopped here before and you look like you know what you're doing.

or *Hi! You look like a smart shopper. I'm lost! Do you know where the bakery section is?*

You can glance in someone's cart and comment:

Wow! That sauce is just the brand I was looking for. Can you tell me where you found that?

Plan B. If you freeze, lightly bump their cart to get their attention. When they turn around, giggle and say: *Sorry! I'm a bad driver today.* or *OOPS! I'm so sorry! I hope I don't get a ticket.*

THE CLOTHING STORE CONNECTION

Imagine a place filled with lighting and color. The energy in the air is calm, yet exciting! When you walk into this artistic, friendly place, people approach you and ask if they can help you. Yes, that's a clothing store and it's also a great place to connect with others!

People shop for clothes all the time and there are so many clothing shops around. These stores are filled with people and new customers enter every few minutes. So the next time you shop for clothes think about the people in the store, too. If you are a woman looking to meet a guy, you'll find plenty of them at men's clothing stores. Plus, men can find a lot of women at women's clothing stores. All these men and women having something in common-shopping! Use that common point as a way to reach out.

You could start a conversation with, "Excuse me, I need to buy a shirt for my brother who is broad shouldered just like you. What do you think of this shirt?" You could also try, "I'm buying a blouse for my sister, and I'm not sure if she'd like this color. What do you think?" People are flattered when you ask their opinion. So ask away. One of my dating students wrote me "This guy asked me if I could help him pick a scarf for his sister-in-law. He was so sweet, I ended up asking him for coffee and we've been dating for months!" Shopping for clothes connects you to people. Why not expect to date and feel great?

Clothing stores are also exceptional places for practicing your flirting. Women are guaranteed to meet dressed-up cute guys at a men's clothing store. I'm talking about the sales clerks! Men can also use this technique at women's clothing stores. If you want to meet a nice woman, go shop at women's clothing stores. It's the job of the sales clerks to reach out and help you!

YOUR SCRIPT

In a clothing store, you could go up to that cute guy or gal and say:

Excuse me, I have to buy a shirt for my brother/sister. You look like you have a great style like him/her. What do you think of this shirt?

or

Gosh, I love that shirt that you're trying on! I'd love to get that for my cousin. Do you mind if I copy your great taste?

or

Excuse me, I need a second opinion from someone with style. What do you think of this sweater?

or

Hi! I need a smart opinion. I'm thinking of getting this scarf for my sister. Would you like this if someone gave it to you as a gift?

or

That sweater looks great on you! Where did you find that? Would you mind if I bought one, too? My brother could use a sharp look like that.

THE PARK PICK-ME-UP

Whenever I'm outside I feel both calmed and exhilarated by nature, don't you? Studies show that spending time in nature gives a sense of inner peace and rejuvenation. So if you go to a park for a little while, you boost your well-being and you could meet someone, too! One gal from class said she took up walking to deal with her frustrations at work. Later she wrote me, "I noticed this guy would go walking the same time I did in the morning before work. After a month we started saying hi, which grew into small conversations. He's so sweet. I might just even ask him out!"

People are in open, receptive moods when they are outside enjoying the weather. If you go to a park alone, seat yourself somewhere in the center where people are hanging out. You want to be visible, so don't sit off to the side, which sends a message that you are an observer. As you sit near the center of things, show you are fun on your own. Look around you and smile. Have a journal to write in, an interesting book to read or bring a radio and play fun music. You can also reach out to people by tapping into their current activity.

If some people are playing Frisbee, you can approach them and say, "Can I try a toss?" If someone has a dog, go up to him/her and say, "What a great dog! Can I pet him?" People love to talk about their pets. You can go to a dog park even if you don't have a dog yourself. Go and watch the dogs! Tell the dog owners you love dogs and you're thinking of getting one in the future. Ask them about their dogs. Just being outdoors and enjoying the park will energize you and lead you to more people!

YOUR SCRIPT

When you go to a park alone, bring a prop like a book, radio, camera or Frisbee. Seat yourself in the center of things. Smile and show you are having fun on your own. Say *Hi* to new people as if you know them. Make positive comments like:

Isn't it the perfect day to be outside?

I haven't played Frisbee in years. Can I try a toss?

I love your dog! Which breed is he?

Excuse me, do you know if this park has a drinking fountain?

I love your roller blades. Did you get those around here?

Hi. I couldn't help but notice your sneakers. What brand are yours?

Excuse me. Would you mind taking a picture of me? I promised my sister I'd send her a nice picture in the park.

THE GYM GEM

He's a superstar who meets Hollywood starlets wherever he goes. He could date famous women and be fixed up with anybody. So where did Jerry Seinfeld meet his wife? When they were both working out at a gym! She went to get some hand weights while he was reaching for them and the next thing you know...sparks! Sometimes our soon-to-be romances are right there in front of us.

Now, there is a myth that when you're flirting for romance, you want to dress for success. Actually, often when you are not dressed up, when you are in casual clothes with no make-up, or for guys, when you haven't shaven, is when you look very appealing with a relaxed image. One great thing about meeting people at the gym is that you have exercising in common with everyone and you chose the same workout facility. You can talk about these things once you've connected. So go to the gym embracing your own attractiveness and reach out to others!

YOUR SCRIPT

At a gym, break the ice by asking for help:

Excuse me, do you know how to program this stair master?

Can you spot me for a second?

Hi! Do you know if this gym has a basketball court?

Cool gym bag! Where did you get that?

Hi! My tennis partner just ran into car trouble. Do you want to hit with me?

THE FIRM FIND

"I sell these awesome knives that make cooking so much easier." That's how I explained my job when I first graduated from college. I sold knives and cutlery sets to people in their homes. Through that firm I met a guy who I dated for awhile. We belonged to the same company, but worked in different offices. We clicked at a regional company gathering, became friends and dated. I liked that we were in different offices, which kept our focus on our work, but at the same time it was fun to have that particular job in common.

Millions of singles meet through work. Since we all spend so much of our lives at our jobs, meeting eligible people through our companies and places of work is, in some cases, an option. It can also be a delicate situation. If your company discourages or forbids inner office dating, then steer clear of dating at work. If your company has no policy regarding inner office romances, then use common sense.

For example, if your corporation is small and you would be running into this person often, then avoid inner office dating. Seeing this person all the time is disruptive whether you are in love or you have just broken up. On the other hand, if your company is very large and you feel you will never run into the person you are dating, then you may consider dating within the company.

Even though you may not be able to date someone at work, you can use your office as a networking service for dating. Tell your coworkers that you are open to being set up, then share the qualities that you are look-ing for in a date. One of my dating students was approached with *The Firm Find.* An office assistant said to her, "I know a guy who I think would be per-fect for you. Are you open to meeting him?" She was open and ended up marrying him!

YOUR SCRIPT

If you have your eye on someone that you've seen occasionally around your firm, you can break the ice with:

Hi! My name is _____. I've seen you in the hallways, but no one has introduced us yet.

or

Hi! I'm _____. I promised myself I'd try to meet more people at the company.

What's your name?

Then you can take it a step further after you've chatted for awhile. Say something like:

The weather is great today. Want to join me outside at lunch?

If a coworker wants to set you up, make sure you know the inner qualities are you looking for.

What would those qualities be?

THE SPORTS SPOT

"I was rooting for my team at a sports bar," one dating student told me, "when this guy from the next table started cheering louder than me. He was all 'Go Vikings!' and I was all 'Go Packers!' We both kept getting louder and louder until everyone at our tables started cracking up. He came over to tell me how his team was going to win. We talked awhile and he asked me out. We dated for three years!"

Sporting events are an excellent way to meet other singles who have similar passions and interests. You can meet other sports fans at actual sporting events like basketball or football games, at pre-game sports activities, at sport bars and even at signings for sports stars. Whether you are a long term fan or seeing a game for the first time, you are all part of an exciting event unfolding in front of you! You may meet someone or discover a new passion. One of my dating students met a great guy at a baseball card memorabilia event. She is a single mom and brought her son, who loves baseball. While standing in line her son started showing his cards to the man behind him and soon they were all talking.

Meeting people at pre-game events is also a blast!

Fans who attend pre-game parties are in a festive mood and are ready to have fun. Sports fans love to talk about their favorite teams, players and what's going on in the current season. When you go to a sports event, you'll be sure to get noticed if you wear something that represents your team-like a special hat, jersey, or even a little face paint. Your team spirit immediately engages other fans!

YOUR SCRIPT

When you are at a sports bar, you can reach out by saying:

Nice play, wasn't that? _____ has so much talent!

or *Did you see that pass? I could watch that replay ten times!* or

Hey, you are a _____fan, too! Who is your, favorite player?

When you are at a pre-game party, you can reach, out with:

Here's to the _____! I've been psyched for this game all week, haven't you?

or *What do you think the point spread will be? I have a guess, but I'm not making any bets.*

or *Cool jersey! Where did you get that? I love it!*

At a sporting event, talk to people nearby or to people you run into at the concession stand: *Great game tonight! Do you have season passes?*

or *We are in an awesome section, aren't we? These games are such a highlight to my week!*

or *I have a feeling we are going to win. I'm ready to celebrate!*

THE PARTY PLACE

She looks like a friendly person, I thought to myself at a party years ago. I was invited to this party by a gal I met from work. I didn't know a lot of people in town since I had just moved here, so the host introduced me to Beth, who also just moved to Minneapolis. Beth and I hit it off! After chatting for awhile she said, "You have a lot in common with my brother. You should meet him. He's in college right now. He's a few years younger than us. When he comes to visit, I'll introduce you. You two could be great friends." Months later I met her brother Joe. He and I did have a lot in common, and we did became great friends. Years later that friendship blossomed into romance. Today Joe is my best friend, my business partner and my amazing husband of over ten years. I'm so glad I went to that party!

Parties are an excellent way to meet other singles. Even if you don't meet someone to date at the party, you could meet people who lead you to other people. Be open to attending work parties, building parties, neighborhood block parties, parties for restaurant or night club openings, charity event parties and more.

Go with an open mind. You don't want to go to a party thinking, I have to meet a potential date tonight. That's too much pressure. Go with the goal to see what you can learn from every conversation. Then you'll have fun no matter what. One dater I coached said, "I went to a work party I was dreading. Then I started chatting with our receptionist. I discovered she knows everything about movies! She was so fascinating that soon more people joined us and we were having a huge group talk about films. It was one of the best parties I've gone to!"

YOUR TURN:

The next time you go to party,

Think: what can I learn from every conversation?

Act: like you already know the people at the party and talk to them warmly.

Imagine: you are famous and people are there to meet you.

YOUR SCRIPT

Approach people and say:

Hi I'm _____. I know a few people here. How about you?

Hi I'm_____. Great turn out! How did you hear about the party?

Hi I'm_____. I love your outfit. Did you find that here in town?

Everybody knows a party is about mingling, so work the room.

If you need to move on from a conversation say warmly:

You are so fun! I admire your passion for _____. I'm going to go mingle a bit. Thanks so much for spending time with me!

THE BAR STAR

"Yep! It's true! We met at a bar," a woman once told me about her relationship. She said, "Just because I like bars doesn't mean I'm a one night stand gal. I saw this cute guy and asked him if he wanted to dance. We talked most of the night. When the bar closed I told him if he wanted to see me again, he would have to ask for my number and he did."

Bars are known for their "singles scene" as men and woman flock to them on Friday and Saturday nights. In the bar scene there is a feeling of flirting awareness. People are checking each other out and looking to meet others. At the same time, bars can also be loud and dark, which sometimes makes it tough to hold a conversation. If you meet someone at a bar, you could suggest to move on to the coffee shop that's next door or down the street.

Anyone can be a *Bar Star* by going to a bar with an open mind. Go with some friends, knowing that your mission for the evening is to have fun with them. If you meet someone new, great. If not, that's okay, too! Keep a healthy attitude and grounded mindset. You don't want to feel desperate or exude desperation either. Hold your head up high, smile, laugh and think empowering thoughts about yourself. If you want someone to approach you, smile at them and face their direction. When your eyes lock, smile!

One more way you can be a *Bar Star* is to protect yourself. If you do meet people you click with, don't go home with them or take them home the first night. You don't know them well enough. Have a second pre-date during the day. Have coffee together or take a walk. See how you feel about them on a second meeting and take your time.

YOUR SCRIPT

At the bar you can use the direct line approach. Remember?

Hi I'm_____. I'm little nervous right now, but when I saw you I knew if I didn't say something, I'd regret it tomorrow.

If you meet someone at a bar you can always say:

Let's go to the coffee shop down the street where it will be easier to talk.

or

It's so loud and dark in here! I'd love to talk more. Want to meet me for coffee some time this or next week? Here's my card. Tuesdays are a good night to reach me.

or

I know a jazz bar nearby which is a little quieter. You want to go there for a bit? It's a cool place and it will be easier to talk.

THE COFFEE SHOP STOP

Need a boost? Go to a coffee shop. You can get a warm beverage and meet warm people. One guy I coached told me he had a crush on a girl who goes to the same coffee shop. He said he wanted to ask her out, but found himself unable to speak in her presence.

He told me, "I'm lucky if I can walk near her without fainting." I told him to remember that he doesn't need to be smooth or clever. Just say something simple to make an initial connection, like asking to borrow a newspaper section off her table or even ask for the time.

The next time he went to the shop he saw her sitting there with a girlfriend. He bought an iced drink and as he walked by her table, he said to the girls, "Excuse me, do you two know what time it is?" They told him the time and that they liked his jacket. They chatted some more. After 10 minutes they invited him to see one of the girl's brother's rock band playing that night!

Coffee shops are filled with people and these days there is a coffee shop on nearly every corner. Many people have success meeting singles in coffee shops. Think about it. A coffee shop is like a social event. People are relaxed. They sit for awhile with friends or they go in alone with a book or a magazine. A coffee shop is comfortable, casual and open for long hours. Try *The Coffee Shop Stop*.

YOUR SCRIPT

When you go to a coffee shop, get a drink and sit down near people. Look around and see if they are reading anything. Is there a newspaper near them? Use this as a reference point. Say:

Are you reading that paper? I love the lifestyle section!

Are they reading a book?

Someone just recommended that book to me. How do you like it?

Check out their drink:

That drink looks so good. Which one is that?

Use your sense of humor:

Do you know what time it is? Oh thanks! I think it's time for a refill. Can I get you anything?

THE CLEANERS CORNER AND THE LAUNDRO-MAT MATCH

She's been married since 1966. That's when singer Dolly Parton met her husband. He spotted her waiting outside of a laundromat! Cleaning our clothes. That's one thing we all have in common. During the week we drop off or pick up clothes at our cleaners. If we don't have a washer and dryer in our house or apartment building, we use a laundromat. These places are excellent for meeting other eligible singles!

A past dating student emailed me about her *Laundromat Match*: "My laundromat has a bulletin board where you can advertise your business. My business card has my picture on it. I walked into my neighborhood laundromat and this guy who was washing his clothes there saw me and said, 'It's you! I've seen your picture on the bulletin board.' We started talking about good times to do laundry and what detergent we use. We ended up doing our laundry together for hours. When we were done I took my card off the bulletin board and gave to him."

I was at my own neighborhood cleaners the other day and asked the clerk if she ever set any of her customers up on dates. She said, "Oh sure, all the time! In fact I have a wedding to go to this weekend. All I did was tell one of my customers that the man she was chatting with at our counter mentioned he liked her. A few months later he came in to tell me they had a great date. And now it's their wedding weekend. I was so flattered they invited me."

One past dating student told me, "I had success with *The Cleaners Corner*! I met the greatest gal. Twice we picked up our cleaning at the same time. The second time I saw her she said hi and that she liked my sweater. When she left I asked the clerk if he knew anything about her. He told me she is single and she works nearby. 'She usually stops by this time every week,' he told me. So I went back again the next week and gave her my card. I said if she ever needs an accountant or just wants to take a walk to call me. She blushed and called me three days later."

YOUR SCRIPT

Next time you go to the laundromat or the cleaners, start conversations with the other customers.

Experiment by doing these errands at different hours and you'll open your world to many different people.

When you want to reach out at the cleaners say:

This is my favorite cleaners. Don't they do a great job?

When you want to reach out at the laundromat say:

Laundry time! If you need any extra detergent I've got plenty.

CHURCH, TEMPLE AND SPIRITUALITY GROUPS: THE WORSHIP WATCH

Do you like to go to Temple or Church? Meeting someone at the place where you worship means that you meet someone with whom you share common beliefs. Groups are always happy to have new visitors and you never know where this new connection will lead.

One woman told me, "One night I visited a singles club at the Temple around the corner from my house. I met some really nice people. One of the girls I talked to was so fun and she told me about her cousin who was also single. She set us up, and we were so happy to have our religious backgrounds in common."

There are also spirituality discussion groups held through bookstores, spiritual centers and more. You can visit a discussion group one time, a few times or for a longer period of time. These groups welcome guests.

I once attended a session of a book club held at a member's home. Even though it was only once, I had such a great time and met so many cool people! At one point I started to share a dream I had: "I was on a boat with other people. I looked towards the front of the boat and there was John Lennon." As I told my dream, I noticed that one woman in the book club looked shocked. When I asked her if she was feeling okay she said, "I had the same exact dream about John Lennon!" Then another woman said, "Maybe John will visit me in my sleep tonight!" Even though I had never met these women before, we connected on a deep level.

Look in your local paper for the groups that meet in your area. Attend one you've been curious about and go with an open mind.

YOUR SCRIPT

Attend one of the singles meetings or discussion groups and tell people:

Hi! I'm_____. I'm a visitor tonight. How long have you been coming to this group? Do you like it?

Go to a book signing for a spiritual author. Say to a fellow attendee:

Hi! I'm so excited to hear this author. Have you read her latest book?

Attend services for a first time visit and say:

I'm really looking forward to the services today. Have you enjoyed the programs here?

You are halfway through this chapter. Keep it going! Life is your 24-hour dating service.

Go for it!

THE HOME ZONE

"My building has this lounge room," a past dating student once told me. "I went to the lounge one Saturday night and I saw the hottest girl there reading a book. I was too nervous to introduce myself. So I went back the next Saturday night and there she was again! This time I asked what she was reading. The next thing you know we were at the nearby coffee shop talking about books. Who knew a great girl was right at my doorstep?!"

In your apartment complex or on your street there are eligible singles. You are bound to run into them often. So if you see someone appealing and you didn't get a chance to meet the first time, you can count on running into him/her again. Take note of which weekday and time you saw him/her. Return next week at the same time and make the effort to say hi.

If you do meet someone on your street or in your building who you want to date, make sure you establish your boundaries from the outset. Once you two have decided that you would like to get together in the future say something like, "Great! just give me a call if you ever want to take a walk or grab a bite to eat." It's important to clarify to call first. Some people will spontaneously come by and knock since you live so close to each other. That kind of dropping by is a bit too close for comfort when you just met. A simple mention of calling ahead of time will let them know you honor each other's space.

You may even meet someone special when you are looking for a place to live. When actress Nicole Kidman was looking to rent an apartment, she checked out rock singer Lenny Kravitz's loft. They met to discuss the living space. The next thing you know, sparks flew between them.

If you use a real estate agent to find a place, let him or her know you are also looking for a great date. You may find more than a house or an apartment.

YOUR SCRIPT

When you see someone in your building who you would like to get to know better, say:

Hi I'm_____. I've seen you around the building. I have lived here a year. Have you lived here a long time? **Once you two decide to take a walk or grab a coffee sometime say***:*

Sounds great! Just give me a call to set that up. Let's exchange numbers.

Meet your neighbors by walking the block during a busy time each day, like when people come home from work around 5:30 p.m. or 6:30 p.m. You will run into the same people, and after a few sightings, you can introduce yourself:

Hi! I'm_____. I see you all the time. Do you live on this street, too? **or**

Hello again! I've seen you so many times. You must also live on this street. I'm_____.

Send the signal to your neighbors that you are approachable. Do outside activities like washing your car, raking your leaves or gardening. When you see a familiar neighborhood face walk by, reach out and say: *"Hey neighbor! Great day, isn't it?"*

THE HAIRCUT SETUP

Don't you just love getting your hair cut?! Next time you get a haircut, think about being setup for a date. One dating student told me, "I did *The Haircut Setup* and told my stylist I had a crush on singer Dave Matthews. I like his looks and I like that he is artistic. She told me she has a client who resembles him and is also artistic. Then she said he has an appointment later that day and I should stop back in. So I did. I came back to buy some shampoo, and she introduced us. When I left he asked her for my number!"

Salons are a great dating service. Next time you get your hair cut, ask your stylist if she has other single clients and if she would be willing to set you up. Describe the inner qualities of the person you would like to meet.

In addition to your stylist setting you up, you can also meet other singles in the lobby of a walk-in hair cutting salon. I go to one of those walk-in salons. I love the idea of getting an immediate appointment. Every time I go to get a haircut I end up talking to someone who is also waiting. Getting a haircut usually puts people in a good mood and you already have something in common. So reach out!

YOUR SCRIPT

When you are waiting in the lobby at a walk-in or by-appointment salon, practice reaching out and meeting the other people who are also waiting. You could say:

Which stylist do you go to?

or

I love getting my hair cut. It's such a mood lifter, isn't it?

or

Your hair looks so good. Did you just get it cut?

For a walk-in place, you could say:

I just realized this morning I needed a haircut. I love how you can just walk in, don't you?

or

It's always busy when I come here. They are so popular, aren't they?

or

We're lucky it's not that busy today. We should get right in.

If you go to a regular stylist, mention to her or him:

If you know anyone who is _____ and
(describe inner qualities)

loves to_____ let me know. I'd love to be set up. (mention a hobby)

or

I love dating and meeting people. Do you have other single clients looking to be set up?

THE CLASSES MASSES

"Life Long Learning." I love that slogan! It's on one of my community education catalogs where I teach classes. Taking classes as an adult is all about enriching your life. One past dating student told me, "I liked the idea of taking classes. I've always been curious about photography so I signed up for a two hour class. I met the nicest girl there and we became friends. A month later she set me up with her cousin. I really like him. The other great thing that happened in class is that I discovered a hobby I love!"

Taking classes is also a win-win. You meet other people with curious minds and you learn something new. Every town and city has an array of community education classes with a range of subjects from photography, goal setting, meditation and so much more. Many of these courses are held one night for a few hours. I love teaching classes through community education. I meet such interesting people from all ages and backgrounds. I admire people who continually work on their personal growth.

Call a community education facility near you and ask them to send you a free catalog. Ask the community education staff which classes attract singles. Scan through the brochure and see what strikes you. You'll feel great about yourself for learning something new and you never know who you may end up sitting next to!

YOUR SCRIPT

If you meet someone you like in class, say to them:

I really enjoyed meeting you. I'd love to take a walk with you sometime or take a different class together. Here's my phone number in case either of those ideas interests you. I'm usually easy to reach on Wednesday nights.

or

You were so much fun in class. Are you taking other courses here?

or

That was a really interesting course! What did you think?

or

Wasn't that fun? I think I'll grab a cup of coffee and look over my notes. Want to join me?

THE BOOKSTORE BET

"Drop your books," I whispered in my walkie-talkie during a *Today Show* appearance. I was coaching a girl at a bookstore. She spotted a guy she liked, but she felt too nervous to speak, so we went on to Plan B. "Just drop the books in front of you," I told her. She dropped her small pile of books. He said, "Let me help you." They kneeled down together to scoop up the books and smiled. Presto! A flirtatious connection.

Bookstores are a fun place to meet other singles. While you're browsing through the store, you can glance through different books or glimpse the latest issue of your favorite magazine. See what other people are reading. You may like to read the same things. One dater from class tried *The Bookstore Bet.* He told me, "I went to one of those mega book store chains. They carry my favorite music magazine from England, *Mojo.* When I got to the magazine section, this girl had grabbed the last copy. I asked her, 'Is that the last copy? *Mojo* is my favorite!' She said, 'It looks like I got the last one. Tell you what. I have some time. Let's go to the coffee bar in here and you can read it until I have to leave.' She was a doll! I didn't even read it. We couldn't stop talking about music. We've had three dates so far. I feel lucky that was the last copy."

YOUR SCRIPT

Go to a bookstore and notice the other customers. What are they reading? Where are they browsing? If someone is reading a book or magazine that interests you, say:

Excuse me. I've been looking for that book. Where did you find it? or

Someone just told me to get that book. Is it good? or

Is that The Flirtologist's Guide To Dating? I read that. It's great!

Looking to buy a gift for a friend or relative? Find the section of books that interests them. Reach out and say:

Gosh, there are so many books about film. I want to get one for my cousin. Do you know of a good one? or

I love films, don't you? I hear this book is really good!

You can also try Plan B. Sometimes you need to take action to make that connection. Drop your books and say: *Whoops! Then thank them when they help you pick them up!*

THE VOLUNTEER VICTORY

I play the guitar for fun, but I haven't played long. I wanted to play in front of an audience, so I volunteered at the nearby senior center at the Salvation Army. I had such a blast! I call it my "Rockin' The Salvation Army Tour!" The seniors are such a sweet audience and they love to sing Beatle songs with me. I go back to play several times a year, and I feel so excited each time! You, too, could use a special skill you have to create a volunteer opportunity.

Volunteering for a day or an afternoon is a great way to meet kindhearted people without making a huge time commitment. Plus you make a big difference and you feel good about yourself! You can find events or organizations to volunteer for anytime. There may be something that's just perfect for you. If you don't want to volunteer alone, go with a friend and try out a place for a couple of hours.

YOUR SCRIPT

Look in your local paper and see what volunteer opportunities are around. Circle the ones that appeal to you. Try one out that requires a small time commitment and see how you like it. At the beginning of the event you can approach someone and say:

This seems exciting. I'm here for the first time. How about you?

or

Wow! What a great turn out. Do you know if it's like this every year?

or

This is my first time at this event. Do you know a lot about this?

At the end of the event, you could continue a dialogue with someone and say:

What a great time I had here today. Are you coming to the next one?

or

Wasn't this a fun event?! How did you hear about it?

or

I'd love to volunteer for more things like this! Do you know of other events like this one?

or

This was really a special day. What was your favorite part? Hey, you want to grab a cup of coffee and talk some more?

THE STREET GREET, CELEBRITY STYLE

Do you know that Nancy Sinatra song that goes, "These boots were made for walking...and that's just what they'll do..." ? Well that's all you need to meet someone. Put on your boots (or shoes) and start walking! Every time you leave your house or apartment, romance can strike.

When I was featured on *Later Today* for a segment about singles in New York, I coached three women in their late 20s who were looking for love. We sent one gal to a clothing store, one to a bookstore and another woman to a barber shop. They flirted at these spots and met guys, but none of the ladies felt particularly interested in anyone. However, when the one woman was leaving the barber shop, she started walking down Fifth Avenue when a guy approached her. She told us what he said: "Excuse me. I've never done this before, but you are so cute, and I have a business dinner and dance this Saturday night and no one to take. Would you be my date?" Then she excitedly told us, "I said yes! Normally I wouldn't think of going out with someone I just met on the street, but he was so sincere. I had a good feeling about him. We've had a few dates already, and I really like him." Upon hearing that, the other two women said, "Let's walk around Fifth Avenue this afternoon and see if more cute guys are around."

Have you ever watched the celebrities walk the red carpet on those awards shows? Everybody recognizes the stars and calls their names: "Goldie! Julia! Dustin!" The celebrities smile and strut the carpet with ease and grace. They stop to talk to fans and reporters and they glow from the attention. Now you can be a celebrity and exude the same glow and excitement!

All you have to do is pretend you are famous. Walk around as if everybody recognizes you. Imagine that people have just told you they loved your last movie or song. Then look them in the eye and smile. You'll put people at ease immediately by reaching out first.

A teacher who took my class tried this method. She told me, "It works! I walked down the hallway the other day and pretended I was Celine Dion. I held my head up high and said hello to everyone. I couldn't believe the reaction! The students and the teachers were exceptionally warm to me. I felt great."

<u>YOUR TURN</u>

Who is your favorite celebrity?

Why do they inspire you and how do they carry themselves?

As you walk down the street, imagine you are famous.

You radiate a magnetic energy!

Hey great job on *The Street Greet, Celebrity Style*! Celebrities are great flirts. I must tell you about some celebrity flirtations I had!

After my first *Oprah* appearance, she came up to

me to shake my hand. I couldn't believe that moment had come! For years I wanted to be on her show and tell her how much I respect her. I had visualized it every day and prepared my own little speech to tell her how much I appreciate her. Now was my moment! As she shook my hand I could barely speak the words, "Thank you, Oprah," when suddenly someone whisked her away! I longed for a few more seconds with her. I couldn't believe I didn't get to give her my little speech! I felt depleted. Then my loving inner voice said to me, focus on what went right. I knew the voice was right. After all, I was just on *The Oprah Show*! It was awesome! Wouldn't you know it? In my moment of gratitude, magic happened. I suddenly felt two fingers wrap around my wrist forming the perfect O. How symbolic! It was Oprah! She was talking to someone else while she held onto my wrist. She held it for like 20 seconds! I felt electric! Even though someone needed her attention, she was also attentive to me with her flirtatious gesture. She made feel so special. Afterwards, I told the producer, "Oprah held my wrist for like 20 seconds!" The producer looked at me with deep sincerity and said, "She meant it!" I held onto my wrist the rest of the day.

When I met Matt Lauer for the first time, he was an anchor on a local New York news show and had been filling in as news anchor on *The Today Show*. After our interview, I told him. "Matt! I want to be on *The Today Show!*" He said, "I'm sure you will. You'll do very well. Will you sign my copy of your book?" He was so encouraging! A year later I was on *The Today Show!* Matt was there too, now as anchor! He entered the green room where I was waiting, and I jumped up, "Hi Matt! I'm Jill Spiegel. We met a year ago when you interviewed me." He walked right up to me and smiled, "Of course I remember you Jill!" I had met him only once before, yet he treated me with the warmth of a good friend. I felt on top of the world!

THE INNER CIRCLE SANCTION

Surrounding yourself with positive people is such a large part of feeling good and radiating warm energy to others. The tricky part is sometimes negative people are members of our family or people we sit next to at work. When I say "negative," I mean people who are unsupportive or draining because of their own fears or pain. Don't take unsupportive comments personally. People always come from their own experiences and outlook on life. If they are unsupportive, it's not that they don't care about you. It's just that they can only advise you from their own belief system.

You can wish these people well, while at the same time protecting yourself. You protect yourself by being polite and kind, but not sharing yourself emotionally with them. That means you may be fond of your aunt, but whenever you talk with her about being single, she says something unsupportive and fearful like, "All the good ones are taken," a statement that is not only fearful, but false. Make a mental note to put your aunt in your outer circle. She can be in your life as you protect yourself by sharing your emotions about dating with other people who are supportive and uplifting. Maybe your aunt is supportive when it comes to your career, but when it comes to romance she's fear filled and makes you feel unsupported. Certain people are great for sharing certain things.

Keep in mind what topics are "safe" to discuss with the people you know. Who in your life makes you feel good about you overall? Your friends? A certain coworker? Your dog? One past dating student told me, "I went to summer camp with this guy when I was 10. 20 years later I ran into him and he said he knows a girl that is like my twin in a girl. He said I had to meet her. So he called her. We all went out for coffee and she is terrific! Even though I hadn't seen this guy for decades, he was still in my inner circle."

<u>YOUR TURN</u>

When you identify the people that help you feel grounded and loved, those people are in your emotional inner circle. Take a moment and think about who in your life is encouraging about dating.

YOUR SCRIPT

Let your inner circle, people who encourage you, connect you to other great people. Tell them: *I'm not dating anyone at the moment. I'm having fun with my (hobby 1) and (hobby 2). But I'm open to meeting someone. So if you know anybody who likes (hobby 1) and (hobby 2,) let me know.*

If someone in your inner circle knows someone they think is right for you, you could meet this person casually for coffee or the three of you could get together as friends or meet at a party. Real friends want to introduce you at your own comfort level.

THE LINE FIND

Waiting in line. Boring? Not anymore! Once you work *The Line Find* and reach out to your fellow line mates you'll just love waiting in line! Lines are the perfect opportunity to meet people who share something in common with you. Whether you're waiting in line at a bank, at a luggage check at the airport, at a discount sale before the doors open, at an event or a concert and more, you share an interest with the people around you. So start talking and reaching out! Remember, life has a way of putting us next to people we are meant to meet.

Once I went with my cousin to see Lisa Marie Presley signing her CD here at the Mall of America. We had to wait four hours just to get in the line for the line to Lisa Marie! So we sat on the floor and started chatting. We started talking to the people next to us and we clicked right away! We talked about why we like Lisa Marie and her music. What stars we would wait in line for. Our favorite concerts. Our favorite movies and TV shows. We had so much fun, the hours just flew by. Once the real line opened we knew we might not see each other in the rush. So even though we brought our camera to take pictures of Lisa Marie, we took a few snap shots of our new group. We exchanged addresses since they were all from out of town. A week later I received a letter in the mail and pictures of our great group. It was signed, "Your line buddy."

I was so happy I had my two minutes with Lisa Marie. She signed my CD, and I told her I thought she was the coolest person. She smiled and said "Thank you." She was such a sweetie! I was also so happy I had four hours with my Line Buddies. They turned waiting in line into a party with great friends!

YOUR SCRIPT

Everyone in line is your Line Buddy. Turn the wait into fun! Here are some ways:

You are in line at a movie:

What did you hear about this film? **or** *I read some*

great reviews! or

Well, the last audience is coming out looking happy. That's a good sign.

You are in line at a bank:

This bank is popular. It's always busy. or

We picked the right hour. Usually the bank is so busy.

You are in line at a discount sale:

I'm ready for a day of great deals. or

I had some great finds at this sale last time.

You are in line at a concert:

This is going to be such a great concert! or

I thought about this concert all week. I can't wait!

SUMMARY PEP TALK

Way to go! You just finished your second chapter. You are doing a super job! Let's review all the options in your 24-hour dating service. Look at the list and check off the places and situations you may find your-self in this week. Are you going grocery shopping? Try *The Grocery Store Catch*! Can you think of anywhere you will be waiting in line? Try *The Line Find*! Maybe you have been thinking of volunteering, but have been putting it off. Now you have extra motivation with *The Volunteer Victory*!

<u>Your 24-hour dating service checklist</u>

The Grocery Store Catch

The Clothing Store Connection

The Park Pick-Me-Up

The Gym Gem

The Firm Find

The Sports Spot

The Party Place

The Bar Star

The Coffee Shop Stop

The Cleaners Corner and The Laundromat Match

The Worship Watch

The Home Zone

The Haircut Setup

The Classes Masses

The Bookstore Bet

The Volunteer Victory

The Street Greet, Celebrity Style

The Inner Circle Sanction

The Line Find

You checked off your strategies. Love it! Now keep this book in your purse or briefcase so you can refer to it anytime. Peek in this guide and review your strategy. You are ready!

Now let's move on to what every dater needs to know!

WHAT EVERY DATER NEEDS TO KNOW!
DATING DO'S AND DON'TS

I'm so impressed with you! You are mastering these flirting and dating techniques. Now that we've talked about some ways to meet and approach people by living our everyday lives, let's take a look at some more dating strategies geared towards singles.

First remember:

DATE SMART AND DO IT YOUR WAY

As your personal Flirtologist, I am in favor of all healthy ways to meet people and date. I've seen people be successful with dating services, Internet chatting, clubs for singles, personal ads, blind dates and more. Some people like approaching people and asking them out. Some people prefer being approached and "courted." All those avenues can work for you as long as you feel comfortable with them and stay grounded. Try the strategies that feel right to you. Always remember, nobody can tell you what is right for you. Only you can figure that out.

One dating student told me, "My friend kept begging me to try her singles group. I really didn't want to. I just know it's not my thing. Instead, I decided to take classes at my community center, and I met some really special people. I've learned that when it comes to dating, I have to go about it my way."

<u>YOUR SCRIPT</u>

If someone wants to set you up or try their dating strategy and you don't want to, kindly say: *That's not my style, but thanks anyway.*

Then be proud of yourself for sticking to your instincts.

In today's modern dating world, daters have several services to help them meet other singles.

There are:

THE DATING SERVICE SPECIAL

THE INTERNET GET

THE CLUBS FOR SINGLES MINGLE

THE PERSONAL AD PIECE

We'll look at these in a minute. First let's explore two subjects that protect us from dating disasters: Flirting with your intuition and talking time to heal.

FLIRT WITH YOUR INTUITION

Intuition plays such a key role in life and in dating. When I was at a party in my single days, this one guy starting talking to me. He was very complimentary, but I had a feeling I should get away from him. Later, I found out he had crashed the party and was the host's recent ex-boyfriend! All of us are projecting energy and receiving energy about each other. When somebody feels "off" to you or something about another person makes you feel uncomfortable, honor that feeling and keep your distance. Just ask yourself, how do I feel? What is my gut telling me about this person? Learn to check in with your intuition at all times.

During one flight, I started talking to the guy seated next to me. He was smiling, but I sensed hostile energy from him. My intuition told me to let him go. I gave him one of my flirting postcards and said, "I'll let you do some reading." Then I left him alone. A week later I gave a seminar and three woman approached me afterwards. One of the them said, "We came to your class because you sat next to our boss on an airplane last week." I remembered that guy who seemed irritated with me. Wow! I thought he didn't like me! Then the woman said, "He hated you. He threw your card in the trash. As soon as he left the office we took it out of the garbage. We all agreed. He's so negative that if he didn't like her, she has to be great. Let's take her seminar."

Your intuition is your wise inner self protecting and

guiding you.

YOUR TURN

When your gut tells you not to talk to somebody, honor that feeling.

If someone you talk to doesn't respond warmly, move on. Your kindness creates a ripple effect and comes back to you.

What has your intuition told you about the people in your life?

To flirt with your intuition ask yourself, how do I feel? What is my gut telling me right now? What would love and wisdom tell me in this moment?

WHEN A RELATIONSHIP ENDS, TAKE TIME TO HEAL

Breaking up and healing from a break up take time. One gal from class said, "I had gone out with Shaun for so long. Even though I was glad we broke up, I still thought about him all the time. Then I met the sweetest guy named Ray and we went on a couple dates. I felt terrible because I really like Ray, but when Shaun would call me or someone would mention his name, I'd just lose it and get all confused. Eventually I had to stop seeing Ray and tell Shaun to stop calling me. I took six months off from dating. I even took a trip alone, and I learned that I'm great on my own! You are so right about healing time."

When you've broken up with someone after dating several months or more, it's important to take time to be single and heal emotionally. You will know you are ready to date again when the person from your last relationship is no longer a habit in your life. That means you've stopped missing their daily phone calls. Their pictures have been put away and you don't think about them all the time like you did when you first broke up.

Be careful of having a lot of contact with your ex. Some people fool themselves into thinking they can be friends with their ex right away. You can't be friends with your ex right away. Maybe down the road. First you have to get used to forming a life without them.

If you have recently broken up with someone, you need time to grieve the relationship. Sometimes you'll feel fine and other times you might feel like calling him or her - or crying. Do the crying. The only way to grieve is to feel those sad feelings and then they pass.

YOUR TURN

When you feel tempted to call your ex, call a good friend instead. Tell yourself that you'll wait an hour. Then you'll see if you still have the urge to call. By the time the hour is up the urge won't feel as strong.

Great! You are using your smarts on the path to dating success! Now let's take a closer look at those dating options I mentioned.

THE DATING SERVICE SPECIAL

You know that appealing singer Paula Abdul? One show business magazine I read said that she tried a dating service. She had dated other celebrities and had her share of romance blues. Then she decided to join a Hollywood dating service and they fixed her up with a "very nice" guy! Dating services are a popular option for today's dater. Every city has dating services available with different approaches. See if you can get some references or talk to people who have gone through the particular dating service you're considering before you sign up. Getting a little background always helps you feel more aware.

Some dating services set up lunch dates and some provide "speed dating," where you meet a new face every few minutes in a gathering for many singles. There are even services that set up dinner parties. Find a service that fits you. One dating student told me, "I tried three-minute dating and it felt like a meat market. I couldn't get a feel for someone in such a short time. Then I tried eight-minute dating, and I really liked that one. I met some great people. Eight minutes was much more my speed."

<u>YOUR TURN</u>

Before you try a dating service, ask for a reference or get a referral from a trusted friend.

THE INTERNET GET

"When you turn on the Internet, you empower your life!" I know a computer buff who made that his slogan. He has a point. Many people have met friends and found love online. You can try a reputable online dating service to meet people or you can also connect with others by surfing the net on subjects that interest you. From there you can join chat rooms about that very subject and meet like-minded people.

One way to be a good "chatter" is to write like you talk. Sound conversational and relaxed. It's also so important to represent yourself honestly during a chat. Don't lie about your age or make up anything untrue about your life. A person who lies about one matter may be less reliable in other areas. Look for people who are honest as well. You can even say in your chat, "I really value honesty in people." After you've spent time getting to know each other online and decide to meet, first tell a friend where you'll be and bring a cell phone if you can. Then meet in a public place during the day so if something doesn't feel right, you can just leave. If it does feel right, have fun!

YOUR SCRIPT

Remember in a chat, highlight your qualities in an inviting way.

Don't say: *My last boyfriend (girlfriend) complained that I never liked to go out.*

Say it like this: *I like to spend time with people who enjoy just hanging out and listening to music. I'm a homebody. What do you like to do for fun?*

THE CLUBS FOR SINGLES MINGLE

Do you ever read your horoscope or glance at the comics? I love doing that! Next time you read the paper also check out the classified ads. You can find current social gatherings for singles. So every few weeks, check the Sunday paper and check the weekday papers, too. Get involved in clubs that promote your interests. From business organizations to political organizations, being with a group of people keeps you meeting new faces and creates purpose in your life. Some clubs are specialized-like clubs for older singles or singles with children. There are even singles organizations that offer schedules with a different activity going on every night of the month. There are also singles clubs built around volunteering or cooking. If you find a club that interests you, you can usually attend one event for free.

One past dating student joined a singles club to fill her nights with different activities. She wrote me, "I didn't meet anyone that I dated, but I had so much fun with all the activities. I also met this sweet girl at the club who I fixed up with my cousin. New people join all the time. So who knows? I could meet someone for a romance, but in the meantime I'm busy and happy."

If you go to a singles club you can always go right up to people, introduce yourself and ask about the club. People love to give their opinion about something they know. Keep in mind that even though regular club members are happy to see new faces, they don't always approach a new face. They are nervous just like you. In one of my classes a woman told the group, "I went to this crowded singles club and no one came up to me." Then this guy in class stood up and said to her, "Hey, I saw you there. You're so attractive, I froze. I was hoping you would come up to me." Try not to judge people's intentions. Instead, think about what you can offer others-like your warm smile, positive attitude and the friendly way you introduce yourself!

YOUR TURN

When meeting people, let go of thinking, *What are they going to think of me?*

Instead think, *What can I offer?*

Then think of your special inner qualities and showcase them!

YOUR SCRIPT

If you try a singles club, go right up to people and say:

Hi! I'm_____. This is my first time here. I'm just checking out different clubs in the area. How do you like this club?

or

Hi! I'm _____. What's your name? This is the first time I've been to this club, how long have you been a member?

Great job on that one!

THE PERSONAL AD PIECE

"I'm a sports buff who loves playing football. I think dates are awkward, but I love going to football games. I don't cook, but I love to order in. Don't call me if you hate football." One dater told me she wrote that no-nonsense ad and met her match.

One way to meet other eligible people and make new friends is through personal ads. They work best when your ad is specific and realistic. Before you write your ad, read other ones to get ideas. You can place an ad and have people call your ad voice mail. Also, you can look through the paper for the ads you may want to respond to.

A recent study on personal ads noted that in big cities women often state the importance of financial stability. A woman in one of my classes once asked me, "Is it okay to say in your ad that you're looking for someone who is financially stable?" The answer is yes. Maybe you've had past experiences where you financially supported a companion and that felt uncomfortable. You've learned that financial stability is important to you. Good for you! The more specific and honest you can be, the better.

Even if you don't think you'll go the personal ad route write an ad for fun. See how you describe yourself and what you're looking for. You may be surprised. One past dating student told me he always thought ads "weren't his style." But for fun he placed a short one. "Nice, quiet guy seeks a nice outgoing girl. My favorite movie is 'Heaven Can Wait.' I like early morning jogs and staying up until midnight." That was it. A few days after he placed his ad, a woman called in and said "Heaven Can Wait" was also her favorite movie. They talked on the phone and months later rented their favorite movie.

<u>YOUR SCRIPT</u>

If you decide to place an ad, make it sound fun while still capturing you.

Instead of: I like Karate movies. Try*: Bruce Lee videos are my favorite.*

Instead of: I like animals. Try: *I love Golden Retrievers.*

All right! Specific examples of your interests bring you closer to dating compatible people.

Now let's imagine you are on the date. Sometimes

it's the little things we do that make a date a big success. In this section we'll discuss crucial dating do's and don'ts to help you feel directed and grounded. If you find you've been doing some of the "don'ts," be easy on yourself. We learn in life as we go along and no one is the perfect dater. If you've been doing a lot of the "do's," be proud of yourself and know that your positive behavior inspires other people!

YOUR TURN

Look at your past dating disappointments as stepping stones to your future happiness. Remember, dating is a learning process.

DON'T IGNORE RED FLAGS, DO LOOK FOR RESPECT

A red flag is an internal warning that something doesn't feel right. Your instincts alert your mind and you feel when something seems "off."

Many years ago I met this guy at work who I liked. I was so excited when we all decided to go out for happy hour so I could get to know him better. When the bill came everybody pitched in except him. He said he forgot he didn't have his wallet. I felt myself think, uh-oh, but I said yes when he asked me out anyway. Wouldn't you know it? After our dinner date he said, "Hey, I only have three dollars on me. Can you pay for the meal, and I'll cover the tip?" I had seen that red flag before and there it was again. It wasn't so much that he didn't have a lot money. I was bothered that he wasn't up front about it. Anyway, my self-esteem was low back then. Despite the red flag, I kept dating him and I nearly went broke!

When you begin dating someone, pay attention to those telling red flags. Your instincts will detect them. Always look for someone who exudes self-respect, respect for others and positive communication. So if you're on a first date with someone who doesn't listen, that's an early sign of poor communication. If your date is very kind to you but rude to the waiter, that's a signal they may not have respect for people in general. The more you practice honoring your instincts the easier it will be for you to see red flags and protect yourself. Think and exude respect and communication and you find it!

Always look for people who possess *The Three Crucial Qualities*:

SELF-RESPECT: A person who has integrity about their life and their decisions.

RESPECT FOR OTHERS: Someone who considers how their behavior impacts other people, cares for others and is kind to

strangers. Look for someone who is loyal to friends and family.

POSITIVE COMMUNICATION: A person who listens, provides empathy and shares their feelings about life with you.

If you find those qualities in a date, you have a foundation for a healthy relationship.

From there you can look for other things you two have in common:

Do you laugh together? Do you share the same interests?

Do you have similar values? Do you feel a physical chemistry?

You deserve to date someone with *The Three Crucial Qualities!*

DON'T MENTION PAST RELATIONSHIPS, DO FOCUS ON CURRENT HOBBIES

"My ex and I used to come to this restaurant." "Hey, let's go to this movie, my ex loved this director." "You remind me of my ex." These sentences are all major don'ts when it come to dating.

Bringing up past relationships on a first date keeps you in the past. It's baggage. The exception to this is widows and widowers who may need to mention their late spouse as part of their healing process. In all other circumstances show yourself and your date that you are in the present moment, which helps both of you fully appreciate the date.

Sometimes all it takes is sharing one area of interest to ignite a great discussion about who you are and what you have in common. One past dating student emailed me, "I was on a blind date and we were both real nervous. We could barely talk. I asked what her favorite radio station was and I turned the dial to her station. This song from the '80s came on and we both started singing and laughing. Then we talked about where we lived when that song was popular. We had a blast from that point on."

When you begin dating someone, explaining your dating history is not the ideal way to help them learn about you. You can show someone who you are by sharing your current passions. The past is the past. Start new relationships with a fresh perspective and celebrate the present!

YOUR TURN

If your mind drifts to past relationships during the date or you find yourself remembering dates from the past, leave those thoughts to yourself.

Say to yourself:

The past is over. I am out with someone new, and I am present in this moment.

Great topics to talk about are your current hobbies and interests and what you like in pop culture, like movies, music, books, etc. Let's think about that right now:

What are your hobbies?

What are your favorite movies and why?

What music has inspired you and who are you listening to lately?

Do you have a magazine you subscribe to or would like to subscribe to?

Have you read a powerful book in the last year?

Do you watch a certain TV show regularly?

Where would you like to travel and why?

Where have you been that you enjoyed?

Do you have a philosophy about life?

DON'T CUT YOURSELF DOWN OR BRAG, BE SUPPORTIVE AND CONFIDENT

Imagine you are on a first date and the guy you're out with says, "I have a degree from Harvard, and I had straight A's. I'm the smartest person in my office. I could do my boss's job a million times better than he does."

When we are on a date with someone who brags about himself it shows his insecurity and distances us from him. People who need to show off are trying to put a mask on their deep need for our validation. So when you are around someone who brags, just say, "Well. I'm your new fan!" You could also say, "I'm impressed!" You'll see how he relaxes immediately now that he's won your approval.

It's also draining when you are on a date with someone who is constantly undermining himself. One dater I coached told me, "This one guy I dated kept saying things like, 'I lost my keys before I left. Gosh I can be such an idiot! I'm like the stupidest person you'll ever meet.' I felt awful for him." Whether showing off or cutting yourself down, both behaviors are extreme and disconnect us from our true self and others.

Here's a great strategy: think confident and supportive at once! "I graduated from Harvard, and I really enjoyed college. I made some great friends there. Where did you go to school?" If you lost your keys before the date you could say, "I misplaced my keys before I left, and I'm so glad I wasn't late. I wouldn't have wanted to take time away from our date tonight." There is always a way to phrase things that make other people feel good about themselves and us. Confident and supportive is the perfect combination.

YOUR SCRIPT

Bragging about or talking against yourself are extreme behaviors that disconnect us from others. On a date, be encouraging to people and speak supportively about yourself.

Complaining too much*: My coworkers and the job itself are OK, but I hate my boss!*

Better*: I like my job, even though my boss is a little challenging. My coworkers are great! Do you enjoy your work?*

Too open*: My family was dysfunctional. My brother had a drug problem, and my dad was a workaholic.*

Better*: There were challenges in my family, but it made me stronger. Are you close with your family?*

Too under confident*: I'm such a couch potato. I'm so lazy sometimes it's scary.*

Better*: I love watching reruns of Seinfeld. George cracks me up! What's your favorite show?*

Confident + supportive = likable, which you are!

DON'T BE RIGHTEOUS, BE CURIOUS

Have you ever been out on a date with someone who needed to be right all the time? One guy told me, "I went out with this one girl who seemed to nit-pick at everything! She would argue with me on the little details. I told her I liked her pin and she corrected me and said, 'It's a broach.' When we were discussing the movie *When Harry Met Sally*, I said I love actresses like Melanie Griffith. She said, 'No! That was Meg Ryan!' This went on all night. When she corrected me she wasn't even nice about it. She seemed thrilled to know all the answers. It was a tough date, and I felt insulted."

Needing to be right at all times is a behavior that disconnects us from people. In all our relationships it's important that we are relaxed about little things. On a date we want to show we are receptive and easy to be around.

In a recent survey of single men, the majority of men said two of the most important traits they like in a date are "agreeable" and "relaxed." Correcting people constantly is neither of those things. Does this mean you have to agree with everything your date says even when you don't? Absolutely not. You still want to be yourself. You can still be respectful without agreeing. So if you disagree with something your date says, respond with interest and a follow-up question. This

way you express your opinion while validating his or
her outlook.

YOUR SCRIPT

**If your date says something you disagree with,
respond with interest and a question.**

Your date says: I love to watch infomercials!

You say: *Hmm. I never thought about infomercials
that way. What is it about them that fascinates you?*

or

**Your date says: I hate animals! They give me the
creeps!**

You say: *Do they? I have to confess, I love animals.
Did you have a negative experience with an animal
or grow up with any pets?*

or

**Your date says: The Rolling Stones are the best
band ever, bar none!**

You say: *I can appreciate that. My favorite band of
all time is The Beatles. Tell me why you love The
Stones.*

MAKE THE FIRST DATE A TIME TO RELATE

Oh my gosh...this movie is so racy! Those were my thoughts during one date. I'll never forget when this sweet guy asked me out in high school. He took me to a just-released movie starring the famous actor Jack Nicholson and acclaimed actress Jessica Lange. I had the sense that my date was excited about these actors, and I assumed this would be a fun date film. The movie was *The Postman Always Rings Twice*. Minutes into the movie the actors were groping and undressing each other! This continued in almost every scene. I could feel that both my date and I were in shock. I felt so uncomfortable, but I didn't say "let's leave" either. It was two hours of tension!

Sometimes people think of a first date as the standard dinner and a movie, but going to a movie on a first date can feel a little intense. You are in an intimate setting, sitting in the dark next to someone you don't know very well. Also, the movie takes hours away from time you could be talking. Plus, you never know when a movie might get awkwardly risqué. Wait until the third or fourth date to see a movie. If you have a meal together on the first date, grab something to eat after you do an activity.

Sitting down for a meal first thing can sometimes feel like an interview. Start the date off with something that keeps you two moving, which helps you feel relaxed. Do something entertaining. One woman I coached told me, "One of my best blind dates was when I went to the botanical gardens for a tour. The flowers were intoxicating and my date and I learned so much about them. It was a special experience."

YOUR TURN

For the first date, choose an activity where you can talk or learn something together. Focus on an activity that keeps the date moving:

Going to the zoo.

Bowling.

Taking a walk.

Playing miniature golf.

Attending an outdoor festival.

Flying a kite.

Touring a nature conservatory.

Walking through a botanical garden.

Painting plates at an art store.

Attending the opening of a restaurant.

ATTENTION COMPULSIVE TALKERS: LULLS AND SILENCES ARE OKAY!

Talk. Talk. Talk. Some people feel they must talk all through a date to keep each other entertained. Talking compulsively on dates usually stems from nervousness as we try to fill in silences with chatter. I used to be one of those people. I'd talk to stomp out silences and then end up blurting inappropriate things like "I napped today and drooled on my pillow!" After such outbursts, I only wished life had a rewind button.

The good news is this is easily resolved. First, we can tell ourselves that silences and lulls during conversations are okay. We don't have to fill the gaps of silence. Just allow yourself a minute of pure quiet, and you'll see that it creates a certain comfort level. One woman told our class, "I was on a great date. We were talking up a storm. Then all of a sudden we hit a lull. It seemed to go on for minutes. I started getting really nervous. I couldn't think of anything to say. I just knew my date was bored. Then after a bit he said, "You're easy to be with."

Being in a quiet space with someone is actually a bonding moment. Paul McCartney said he knew he was falling in love with Linda when he apologized for being tired on one of their early dates. Linda responded casually, "It's allowed." She gave him permission to relax and be quiet. Paul thought, "I like that!"

YOUR TURN

Next time you are on a date and there is a moment of silence, count to five slowly in your head. That gives you time to explore if you are saying things

out of feeling compulsive to fill space or if you are speaking from a purer place. You'll see the quiet was no big deal. It was even relaxing.

Try it now:

ONE TWO THREE FOUR FIVE

Awesome! You are doing so well on what every dater needs to know. Let's take this to the next level and look at some of the "trickier" aspects of dating. As a Flirtologist, I receive a lot of questions. Let's explore them!

TALKING ABOUT SEX ON THE FIRST DATE? A MAJOR DON'T

I am always amazed when people in my dating classes tell me that they've had first dates who have brought up the topic of sex. They feel taken aback when their date asks something like "How many people have you been with?" Some daters mistakenly believe that bringing up sex will arouse their date, but it usually turns them off. One guy told our class, "I was on a date with a woman, having a pretty decent time. We went to an art exhibit and then to dinner. While we were discussing the exhibit, she told me she lost her virginity in a museum. I felt really uncomfortable at that point. I couldn't tell if she was teasing me or what?"

Comments about sex and intimate sexual questions on a first date are extremely inappropriate and crossing major boundaries. When someone attempts to cross this line with us, we have the opportunity to demonstrate self-respect and manners.

YOUR SCRIPT

If someone asks you about sex on the first date, just smile politely and draw your boundaries. Any of the following responses will work:

I don't talk about sex with someone I barely know.

Next subject.

You are kidding right? I know you are much more polite than that.

Then change the subject. (Still, do make a mental note of that red flag.)

WHY DO PEOPLE DATE JERKS?

When I was the expert on a talk show exploring the topic of women dating jerks, the host asked me, "Why would these appealing young women date men who treat them so badly?" I explained, "These women think, 'If I can get this guy to love me then I'll prove to myself I'm lovable.'"

Often we unknowingly try to heal our childhood

wounds through the people we date. For instance, if we felt our parents didn't love us unconditionally or they were overly critical of us, we will pick someone who makes us feel the same way. We crave healing our wounds, hoping we can change these people and prove to ourselves we are worthy of unconditional love. We also gravitate towards what feels familiar, even if it feels bad. That's why I say again how important it is to always make your self-esteem your hobby. Practice self-awareness. Observe the choices you make and try to understand why you make these choices. Work on treating yourself so well that you attract others who will do the same!

YOUR TURN

Think about your childhood role models. Did they have healthy, loving relationships?

Look at your dating choices. Are you re-creating familiar patterns?

Are your dating choices in your best interests?

Love yourself properly and attract healthy love into your life!

WHO PAYS ON A DATE?

There was a time when the man always paid for the date, but times have changed. As more and more women are asking guys out, the issue of who pays is no longer obvious. In today's dating scene, the person who did the asking out is usually the one who pays. At the same time, a polite, considerate dater will always offer to pitch in something. For example, if one person is buying dinner, then the other person on the date can offer to pay the tip or offer to pay for another part of the date. Say, "You paid for dinner. Let me buy the gallery tickets." One guy expressed to me the sentiments of many men, "Even when I want to treat for the entire evening, I always appreciate a woman who offers to pitch in. It tells me a lot about her character."

So what do you do if the person you date has a lot more money than you? Then provide for him/her in other ways. Offer to cook a meal and bring it on a picnic. You could also offer a night where you rent his/her favorite movie. How about suggesting going to a free outdoor concert or visiting a dog park? These are activities where no money is required. The most unhealthy thing a dater can do when it comes to paying is not be up front about it. Let your date know your budget constraints ahead of time. Don't spring it on him/her during the date. When your date pays, make sure you are appreciative. Think mutual respect and fairness. One guy who called in my radio show said, "No matter who asks who out, I think both daters should come prepared to pay. Play it safe."

YOUR SCRIPT

Attention women:

If you ask a guy out, expect to pay. Always show appreciation when you are treated on a date.

If a guy asks you out and the date is not going well for you, say:

Let's split the bill.

If a guy asks you out and you like him, let him pay, but offer to pitch in. Say:

Thanks, what a great meal. Let me get the tip!

or

Thanks! What a fun concert. Let me pay for the parking.

or

Next time I'll take you out.

Always be appreciative that he paid.

WHAT DO YOU SAY WHEN A BAD DATE CALLS FOR A SECOND DATE?

"I thought the date was terrible, but apparently he had a great time. I couldn't believe it when he called me back for a second date," a woman told us in my dating class. It happens. Two people go on a date together and interpret the whole evening differently. If they call you to go out again and you don't want to, be gentle and honest as you say no. Here's an effective answer, "Since our date, things have shifted in my life so I'm going to pass on a second date. I'm glad I met you and I wish you the best." I like this response because it puts closure on the situation without being hurtful.

You don't have to say to someone, "I felt zero attraction to you," or "There were no sparks for me." Saying "things have shifted" is enough. Don't leave the door open by saying, "Maybe later." If they ask what happened, just say, "Oh, it's a long story. I'm not going to get into it." Then wish them well and be on your way.

YOUR SCRIPT

Gently say no to a second date with:

Since our date things have shifted in my life so I'm going to pass on a second date. I'm glad I met you and I wish you the best!

If they ask what happened, just say:

Oh, it's a long story. I'm not going to get into it. Take care now!

No matter how gentle we are with people when they

feel rejected, they may also feel hurt, which they express as anger. One guy I coached told me, "I went out with this girl. We had an okay time, but I knew I didn't want a second date. I didn't kiss her or tell her I'd call her. Anyway, she called and asked me out on a second date. I told her things had changed in my life so I had to pass on another date. All of a sudden, she starts screaming at me and calling me names. I felt terrible! I tried to say I'm sorry, but she hung up on me." If someone lashes out at you after you gently say no, just let them. They are entitled to feel hurt. That doesn't mean you should feel guilty. Everyone processes things in their own way.

YOUR SCRIPT

If a dater lashes out at you for not wanting a second date, calmly say:

Well, I guess we're on the same page. Take care. Bye now!

They will heal and move on. Congratulate yourself for being direct and gentle. Then make sure you move on, too.

I can see you are taking this all in. Excellent! Keep going.

CAN A WOMAN CALL A GUY TO THANK HIM AFTER A GREAT FIRST DATE?

Many women have asked me if it's okay to call a guy and thank him after they've had a great first date. Guys can be very flattered to get a call of thanks. At the same time, if the guy specified he'd call you, then let him. If he doesn't, move on. Otherwise, if you feel the date went really well and you want to call and thank him, then call once and let go. If he answers, tell him you had a great time and you called to thank him. If his machine picks up, thank him on the machine and then let go. In this age of caller ID, where people can tell who called, it's best to leave a message rather than just hanging up. After you've made the call, the letting go is the key part. Remember, you tried once and if he didn't call back, he wasn't right for you for whatever reason. Even if you really liked him and had hopes for more, trust that the universe has a better plan for you. Congratulate yourself for taking chances and moving forward!

One woman told me, "I went on this fun date and this guy took me to an expensive restaurant. So I called a few days after the date and thanked him. I thought we had a good talk, but I never heard from him after that. I was crushed! A few months later, I met someone else, and I realized how much more we clicked than my last date. I ran into the first guy one year later and he was holding hands with another guy. I realized you can never guess why someone doesn't call back."

YOUR SCRIPT

If you feel the date went really well and you want to call and thank him, then call once. Be upbeat, specific and appreciative. Say: *Hi _____, It's _____. I just wanted to call and thank you for a great time! Bowling was really fun even though you beat me! I'd love to do it again sometime. Thanks again, _____!* **After you've called once, let go. Let him call you.**

BE IN THE SELF-RESPECT ZONE, DON'T WAIT BY THE PHONE!

A good date is exciting! You want to go out again, and you hope he/she calls. The tricky part is not waiting by the phone. The moment you rearrange your life to be near the phone, in case he/she calls, is when you lose yourself. Go on with your life! Continue to make your self-esteem your hobby and if he/she calls you when you're out, you'll call him/her back.

A woman in class told us, "I had this incredible date. He said he'd call. A week passed by and still no call. I grew desperate. I canceled my plans the next few weeks in case he tried me. My friends were really concerned about me. Finally, after three weeks I gave up. I started living my life again. It was painful to see how I lost myself, but I'll never sacrifice my self-esteem again."

<u>YOUR TURN</u>

Vow to yourself to never wait by the phone. Don't let your happiness depend on a date's response. If you are meant to be together, everything will work out.

WHAT ABOUT THE LUST FACTOR?

You feel tingly. Your passion is ignited! Sexual energy and lust are exciting. So what happens if you really click on that first date and you both lust for each other? When to be sexual with someone is your own decision. Something to keep in mind is the different effect that sex has on men and women. Studies show that when women have been sexual with someone, they almost immediately feel addicted to them and crave the man's smell, touch, even the sound of their voice. Not so for men. A man can be sexual with a woman and easily detach emotionally from her afterwards. A woman once told me, "I decided I could have this harmless fling with this younger guy I met. Then as soon as we were physical, I found myself wanting to spend more time with him. I was surprised by my own reaction." A guy told me his story, "I had a platonic girlfriend who was such an awesome friend. One night we were intimate and ever since then she wants to be more than friends. I wish we could go back to the way it was."

YOUR TURN

Remember: Lust is intoxicating for both men and women. However, women get attached, while men can maintain distance.

People have also asked me, "If the chemistry is off, can we learn to kiss better together?"

If partners are open and willing to work on their kissing chemistry, yes. Actor Harry Hamlin and his wife, actress Lisa Rinna, said their kissing was mismatched at first, but they worked on it and created great kissing chemistry and two daughters!

BEING BOLD VS. CHASING

True or False? Men usually feel flattered when a woman asks them out. True! Most men tell me they would love it if a woman asked them out or called them first. I had some wonderful relationships that started that way. One time I dated a guy who told me my personality was too assertive and said he liked to do all the pursuing. We were a mismatch. Holding back just wasn't me. Having said all that, I also believe you can go to an extreme and become someone who chases guys. It's one thing to ask a guy on a date. It's another thing to call him every night.

Think self-respect and walk down that path. If you

like to be pursued, then let someone pursue you. You can still make your date feel special with compliments and kindness. If you like a certain guy and want to date him, go ahead and ask him out. Then after the first date, let him ask you for the next one. Go within and ask yourself, does this feel mutual? Is one of us always making more effort than the other? Do I feel respected and am I showing self-respect?

YOUR SCRIPT

If you asked a guy out on the first date and you want a second date, playfully say to him:

If you want to see me again then it's your turn to ask me out on the next date.

HOW FAR IN ADVANCE SHOULD YOU ASK SOMEONE OUT?

"I met a guy I really liked at the grocery store," a dating student once told me. "I gave him my number and he waited a week to call me. When he did call, it was on Saturday morning and he asked me out for that night. That seemed like a little short notice to me." When someone asks us out within one or two days of the planned date, it feels a little disrespectful. As this woman said, "He must have assumed my Saturday night would be open." If you want to take someone out on a Friday or Saturday night, call him or her the Sunday or Monday before. Show them they are a priority to you and that you respect their busy schedule. What do you say if they call you less than two days in advance? You can be polite and interested without being a pushover. Tell them you're busy this weekend, but available next weekend.

Set your boundaries early on and you'll set the tone for the relationship too. When it comes to calling someone after he/she gave your his/her number, call the next day or at least within three days. Waiting a week sends a signal of little interest.

YOUR SCRIPT

When calling to ask someone on a date, call a week in advance. If someone calls you three or less days in advance for a date, tell him/her you're busy and offer the next weekend. Say:

Wow. I'd love to go out with you, but I already have plans this weekend. I am open the following Friday if that works for you.

When you get someone's phone number, call the next day or at least within three days.

SHOULD YOU GO ON A SECOND DATE WITH EVERYONE?

Don't force yourself to have a second date if the very thought of going out with this person again feels drain-

The Flirtologist's Guide To Dating

ing or like a chore. At the same time, if you had an okay time on your first date and you found this person to be pleasant, you could certainly try a second date. After a second date, if you still feel "mild," then you can be proud you were open-minded, but you may want to pass on the third date.

In my single days, I tried a second date with a guy I thought was really sweet, but I sensed there was little chemistry between us. Some people told me, "Try a third date. You're too picky." Actually, picky is important when it comes to romance. I call it being selective. It's your life. Don't settle. Always listen to your inner voice. Evaluate each experience by your own feelings.

<u>YOUR TURN</u>

Mental note: If the first date was pleasant, but had no spark, you could try a second date. If the second date leaves you feeling as mild as the first, you may want to pass on the third date. You can usually sense if the chemistry is right in the first couple of dates.

IS BLIND DATING FOR EVERYONE?

There are millions of blind date success stories, but blind dating is not for everybody. As one woman I coached explained, "I'm a terrible blind dater. I can tell in the first few minutes if I'll want to kiss someone. So when a guy comes to my door and I feel there's no kiss potential, I just lose my zest to go on with the night. Does that makes me a bad person?" Of course it doesn't, but it does mean that this particular person should not be blind dating.

Only try the blind date method if you can go with an open mind and look at the date as an adventure.

When *Today Show* correspondent Jill Rappaport wanted to set up her friend Christie Brinkley with her architect, Peter Cook, she knew Christie wouldn't like the idea of a blind date. So Jill invited Christie over and then had Peter stop by to help with Jill's house. Jill said, "Their eyes locked." Now they're married. Jill was smart to set up a blind "meeting" first.

YOUR TURN

Sometimes you can ease the blind date jitters by having a triple coffee instead. It's a quasi-blind date. Have the person who wants to set you up on the blind date meet with you and the other dater for an informal coffee.

If you meet a blind date through an email, you can always have a friend come with you for the first face-to-face meeting.

Blind dates are all about attitude. Go with an open mind. Look at the date as an adventure. Be proud of yourself for taking a chance! If the idea of blind dating turns you off, don't do it.

DO SENIORS LIKE TO DATE?

I was waiting for a haircut once when a senior gentleman walked in. We started chatting, and I gave him my flirting postcard. He said, "I'm 86 and I'm still a great flirt. I was going with a young gal of 77 for awhile, but she dumped me. She wanted to get married, but I didn't want to get married again. I was married for 50 years. I'm going to play the field for awhile."

Desiring romance and companionship is something we never outgrow. Finding a companion who excites you at 70 can be just as thrilling as when you are 20. What's easier about dating when you are older is that older daters are often direct and in touch with what they want, which is mainly to enjoy life with someone else.

YOUR TURN

Some ways to meet other seniors are through senior recreational trips, dances, senior centers, retirement clubs, through friends and family and senior single clubs.

IS LOVE AT FIRST SIGHT REAL?

You see someone across the room. Your eyes meet. You feel a rush of excitement and an immediate connection! Is it love at first sight? It could be "intense like" at first sight or extreme interest at first sight. Real love takes more time.

Love happens after you truly know someone, understand them and care about their well-being. Love is built over time, while love at first sight is an overwhelming attraction. People often feel these powerful attractions at their first meeting.

When actress Nicole Kidman met actor Tom Cruise, she said it was instant "lust and trust." When I first met my husband I felt drawn to him, and I commented to his sister, "He's so cute I could marry him!" Famous broadcaster Howard Cosell asked his wife to marry him on their very first date and they were deeply in love until "death did they part." It may not be love in the first few seconds, but a magnetic pull toward the other person can mean you sense a special chemistry or connection. John Lennon and Yoko Ono said they felt an instant mind connection when they first met.

People who believe in reincarnation feel that the phenomenon of love at first sight is our reconnecting with a soul we've been close to in many other lives. Whatever the explanation, when you think you are feeling love at first sight, it's a sign your interest is heightened. Continue to love yourself so that healthy, true love can develop with this person if it's meant to be a relationship.

<u>YOUR TURN</u>

Love at first sight is a sign of instant attraction. Wait until at least two dates to decide if this was a brief flash of excitement or a sign of a special connection.

DO FIRST IMPRESSIONS CHANGE?

Is it possible to fall in love with someone who once turned you off? The answer is yes. There are many happy couples who weren't thrilled with their partners at first.

Happily married actor and funny man Will Smith said his wife Jada thought he was "corny" when they met during an audition. Years later they fell in love and married!

When we first meet someone, we may only be seeing a small part of their personality or we may be at a place in our lives where our personalities don't mesh. One email I received said, "10 years ago I went on my first and only blind date. I had a terrible time. Five months later I went to a party and ran into him. This time I felt so differently about him." Although every relationship is different, they all need time and understanding.

YOUR TURN

Review your relationships and friendships.

What were your first impressions?

What were your thoughts as you got to know the person better?

HOW DO I KNOW IF SHE'S SERIOUSLY FLIRTING?

"I like this girl at school and we flirt a lot but I don't know if it's friendly flirting or if it means something serious and I was wondering if you could tell me the difference between friendly flirting and serious flirting. Is there a sure way to tell if someone really likes you?" That was an excerpt from a letter I once received from a high school student.

This young man shares the sentiment of many daters. When are people just being friendly and when are they interested in romance? Here are some questions to ask yourself: Does she or he flirt with you more than they do with others? Do they make an extra effort to see and talk to you? If they are friendly to you in the same way that they are with everyone, then that would tell me they're serious about being friendly.

Sometimes it's hard to know for sure if someone is interested. So if you are not sure, take a chance and ask them out for a coffee or a walk. Suggest something casual and say, "I'd love to spend more time with you." If they feel romantic about you, they'll say yes. If they don't, they'll say no, but they will be flattered. If the answer is no, then congratulate yourself for taking a step towards your happiness. Remind yourself you are that much closer to meeting the right person, and you made someone's day!

YOUR SCRIPT

If you can't tell if someone is interested in you, take a chance and suggest something casual: *I'd love to spend more time with you. How about a coffee or walk sometime?*

Some of the signs that people are interested in you are they primp by fixing their hair or adjusting their clothing. They are fully focused on you. Their eyes, feet and shoulders are turned toward you. Their pupils look dilated when they look at you and you feel a warm energy between you!

WHY DO PEOPLE SAY *I'LL CALL YOU* WHEN THEY DON'T MEAN IT?

It happens to all of us. People say they'll call us, but they never do. There could be several reasons this happens. Sometimes they intend to call, but events in their life change. A past girlfriend or boyfriend comes back into their life or they learn at work they have to move.

It could be anything. They could procrastinate calling for so long that they feel it's too late. Other times people say, "I'll call you" in the way that some people say, "Let's do lunch." They don't mean it, but they think it sounds polite. It's more polite to end a date truthfully, "Thanks. Take care!"

YOUR SCRIPT

When people say they'll call and don't, say to yourself:

That person wasn't right for me. I'm one step closer to finding the right one.

WHEN YOUR BEST FRIEND IS OBSESSED WITH GUYS (OR GIRLS)

"Every breath you take...Every move you make...I'll be watching you." You know that song? Some people think it's about love. Sting, who wrote it, said it's about obsession. At times we confuse the two. While romance and companionship are natural desires, people may turn this desire into an obsession. I often hear from women who have an obsessed friend. When describing this type of friend, one woman told me, "We can talk about everything, but when it comes to guys, she spirals and gets dramatic. I really love her, but I hate focusing on the guy thing so much. Our discussions always go in circles with no resolution. I'm sick of talking about guys, but I don't want to ruin the friendship." It's important to remember you can still love your friend and be a good friend to her without discussing this subject. You need to draw your boundaries and protect yourself. You can do that in a kind way.

The next time an obsessed friend brings up guys, just tell her you're taking a break from that subject. Then bring up something else. Tell her that talking about guys feels draining to you right now and you want to focus on other things in your life. Role model self-respect and you will inspire yourself and others.

<u>YOUR SCRIPT</u>

When a friend is obsessed with dating, tell them:

I'm taking a break from talking about dating right now. How is your work going?

IS BEING FRIENDLY SENDING MIXED SIGNALS?

"My husband is the greatest!" I once told a guy sitting next to me on an airplane. Then to my amazement, this guy suggestively said to me, "When we land you want to have a drink?" I told my husband what happened and that I was sure I didn't give this guy mixed signals. Joe said, "Just remember. Every guy hopes to 'score.'" Women want that, too, but a lot of guys are wired to think of it first and foremost. In fact, guys are so flattered when a woman gives them attention that they immediately feel drawn to her. Even though a man may not be sure that a woman is interested in him, he's hoping that her friendliness is a sign of interest so he asks her out. That's one consequence of being warm and outgoing-you are very popular! You can still be friendly and draw your boundaries.

YOUR SCRIPT

When you are just being friendly and someone asks you out, say:

Oh, I'm flattered, but I'm seeing someone. Thanks!

or

My life is too busy for dates these days. Thanks for the compliment!

ARE YOU STILL SINGLE? AND WHAT'S NEW?

Have you ever felt pressured about your dating status? It happens to a lot of single people. One guy wrote me, "I am in my 30s and have been single for many years. I try to date, but it's hard to meet people. I know this married friend of the family who I always see at family functions. Every time I see her she anxiously says, 'Are you still single?!' It makes me feel awful! I'd love to be in a relationship, but it's not that easy. How do I answer her without adding more shame or apologizing for the situation?" Sound familiar? Even a simple question like, "What's new?" or "What did you do this weekend?" can be tough when you are single.

Keep this in mind: Dating is hard for everybody. Never let somebody make you feel bad about being single. One woman told me when people ask her if she has a boyfriend, she says "No. Do I need one?"

Many people love being single. It's a very precious time in life where you get to explore yourself. So when you are faced with a tacky question, don't take the comment personally. People who pressure you about dating are living in fear and role model fear. You can role model strength and abundance back to them by holding your head up high and smiling. Not letting them get to you will inspire you and their fear will no longer deplete you!

YOUR SCRIPT

Tacky question: Are you still single?

Answer: *Yes, I'm having a great time. I'm busy with my jogging and my art (insert your hobbies). I love my life! What about you? Have you taken up any hobbies lately?"*

Pressure question: So? Any dating news? What's new?

Answer: *What's new with me? Well, I love my new hobby, and I'm enjoying my freedom. What's new with you?*

For close friends, say: *I can tell you are concerned about my dating life. Don't worry, I'm happy. If something happens in my love life I'll be sure to let you know.*

Great job on those tricky parts of dating! Now let's talk about soulmates and how to draw them to you.

THERE ARE SEVERAL SOULMATES FOR YOU

"I think I met my soulmate a few weeks ago, but I forgot to give him my number," a dating student once said to me. I told her not to worry. If someone is truly your soulmate, you will find each other and be together when the time is right. Let the universe take care of it and trust that life is abundant. You get so much more than one chance for things. You get infinite chances!

It's also important to remember that there will be many soulmates in your life. You can have several romantic soulmates and soulmates in friendships as well. A soulmate can be a friend, a parent, a pet. A soulmate is a being that brings you tremendous love, comfort, guidance and a deep connection. Sometimes a soul mate is meant to be in our life for a certain period of time and sometimes for the rest of our life. Even if you lose contact with a soulmate, you will forever be touched and changed by his/her presence in your life!

YOUR TURN

As your dating journey unfolds, remind yourself that there are several soulmates for you. Trust the universe to bring them to you when you are ready.

If you had some tough relationships in the past, look at those experiences as your *Soulmate Boot Camp*. The universe was preparing you to know and love yourself so you'll be ready for the positive soulmates that come into your life.

THE SOULMATE LIST

Here is a fun exercise that helps you draw your soulmate to you. Take out a piece of a paper and make a list of all the qualities you are looking for in a soulmate. Make sure the qualities, you list are inner qualities like someone who loves nature, is patient and kind with people, is a homebody and so on. Stay away from superficial qualities like must have brown hair, drive a Porsche, be exactly four inches taller than you. Be careful not to make the list too long, like a 100 things. A list of 10 to 20 qualities is reasonable. Don't be afraid to write things on your list like, "must be crazy about me." Even though that might be a given, we all want our partners to adore us. Writing what you want and deserve makes you feel strong immediately!

Another reason the list is magical is it sets your intention on paper and into the universe. It's similar to putting in your order at a restaurant. The universe picks up on your intentions and delivers your wish. Plus, the list helps you feel focused as you notice and attract what you desire.

YOUR TURN

Imagine what you want and deserve. Write your soulmate list now.

THE SOULMATE LIST WORKED FOR ME

When I wrote my first soulmate list, I wasn't true to my inner self. In fact, I wrote down superficial qualities like, "must be at least four years older than me". I thought someone older meant more mature, but I soon learned that wasn't true. My husband is actually four years younger than me, yet more mature than a lot of the older guys I dated. I also wrote that my soulmate must take me out to nice dinners. That was something my parents always did for me, but the truth is I am a homebody who loves to eat in, so that didn't fit me at all. My list was disconnected from my true self because I was disconnected from me.

Of course, once I made that list, I attracted that person into my life. He fit those qualities I wrote down and it was a very dysfunctional relationship. When I finally ended that painful relationship, I realized how much I had grown from having gone through it. I saw how I needed to go through that experience to discover my real self! The universe gently gives you people and situations that help you grow and evolve.

After that dysfunctional relationship, I went back to my original soulmate list and looked it over. I couldn't believe some of the stuff I listed! So I crossed off the superficial stuff and added things like "maturity, consistency, integrity." When I looked at the new list, I said out loud, "I know this person! The person on my list is my great friend Joe Brozic!" I ended up marrying my soulmate Joe, who was my good friend for years before we even kissed! He was always in my life. I just needed to grow and go through certain experiences before it was time for us to be together romantically.

<u>YOUR TURN</u>

Honor your *Soulmate List*. Keep it in a special place like your jewelry box or your wallet and trust that the universe is delivering your order like magic!

EMAIL YOUR *SOULMATE LIST* TO ME OR A FRIEND

Now that you've made your *Soulmate List*, put it out to the universe. You do that with your thoughts, which are the blueprint for your destiny!

Another way to give power to your list is to put it in cyberspace, an infinite dimension. Email your list to me at Jill@Flirtnow.com or send it to a friend. We can read the list as we imagine you connecting with your soulmate.

Email your *Soulmate List* now

Great job! Didn't that feel good? Now let's talk about some more ways to feel good. No relationship can ever make you truly happy if you are not happy on your own first. In this next section, let's talk about ways to celebrate yourself and your life every day. These ideas will enhance your life and enrich your relationships.

But first, one quick summary!

SUMMARY PEP TALK

Another chapter done! You are terrific! All of your knowledge and energy you put into this is already paying off for you and will more and more! Now let's take a look at some of the key points from this chapter.

* Make sure you approach dating your way! Whether you try a dating service, the Internet, personal ads or singles clubs, talk to people who have tried out these methods, then decide if they are right for you. Don't let anybody tell you how you must go about dating. Listen to your instincts.

* When you are on a date, always look for someone with *The Three Crucial Qualities:* self-respect, respect for others and positive communication. Don't ignore red flags or mention past relationships. Talk about interests and hobbies. Be confident and supportive. Remember that lulls are okay. For the first few dates, choose an activity that keeps you moving, like bowling or going to the zoo. Keep in mind the one who did the asking out pays, but offer to pay for the tip and always be appreciative.

* If someone calls you for a second date and you don't want to go out with him/her again, be polite and have closure. Don't mislead people with a "maybe another time" suggestion. A woman can call a guy and

thank him for a great date, but be sure to call only once and then let go. Don't wait by the phone hoping to get a call. Live your life!

* Remember the dynamics of dating. Woman often become attached to a guy once they've been physical. Men are able to maintain distance more easily. Guys like it when a woman asks them out, but they don't like being chased. Being friendly is not sending mixed signals, at the same time, people often feel drawn to a friendly person.

* There are many soulmates that will come into your life. To attract a romantic soulmate, make a list of all the inner qualities you are looking for. Read the list from time to time. Live a full life. Trust that the universe is working with you! Be your own best friend.

Great! Now let's go to the last chapter, on making moments into magic!

TURN MOMENTS INTO MAGIC!
CELEBRATE YOUR LIFE EVERY DAY

LOOK AT DATING SPIRITUALLY

There is one person who will be with you forever...you. Being kind to yourself and looking at dating spiritually is a major key to finding happiness in dating. Now, when I say "spiritually," I mean that everyone's journey is unique and everything happens for a reason. Some people are meant to date one person for a long time. Some people are meant to date many people. But everyone can find romance and companionship. When you look at dating spiritually, you feel good about who you are. You attract positive people into your life. You know you are special regardless of your dating status. You have hope and patience.

One way to practice developing a spiritual outlook is to live your life as if everything happens for a reason. Even if you date someone for many years and break up, that experience is a success because you learn from every relationship. No experience or time spent with anyone is a "waste." Every relationship helps you grow and prepares you for your next evolution. If you have been single a long time, the universe is protecting you. Life has a way of knowing what is best for us. Our wishes magically come true when the time is right!

YOUR TURN

You always grow and succeed at dating when you look at dating this way.

Dating is:

Collecting experiences.

Meeting people.

Making friends.

Learning about yourself.

Look back on the relationships and conversations you've had in the past.

What did they teach you about yourself?

How have they shaped who you are today?

Trace the path of your life experiences.

See how everything you went through has helped you evolve as a person and prepare you for the "right" companion.

One date, even one conversation, can teach you a lot about yourself and life.

Be proud of yourself for being open to people and value every experience as part of your unfolding journey.

Every experience you've had has helped you be you. Way to go!

EMBRACE PEOPLE WHO VALIDATE YOUR JOURNEY

One way to build faith in your dating journey is to look at other role models who validate your experience. You can find role models through people you know or through well-known people. Even celebrities struggle with dating. Gwen Stefani from the rock group "No Doubt" is known for her tremendous allure. People assume that she has had millions of dates and a lot of boyfriends. In reality, she has had two boyfriends and she married the second one.

Some people aren't meant to have many dates and relationships. Some of us have sensitive souls, so many dates and a lot of relationships can be too emotionally draining. All it takes is meeting one or two people you connect with.

What if you are in your 50s or older and feeling discouraged about love? Think of Barbra Streisand. After she turned 50 she said she believed that "love had passed me by." Then she went to a dinner party and was seated next to her future husband. It's never too late for love!

YOUR TURN

When you feel discouraged, think of a role model and tell yourself:

My journey is unfolding the way it's meant to. My life is filled with possibilities!

YOUR *INNER CIRCLE/OUTER CIRCLE PLAN*

"I have a cousin who always tells me I better get busy and ask more girls out or I'll end up alone. He keeps pushing me. It drives me nuts!" That's what a dating student once told me. I told him to communicate with his cousin and say, "I know you are looking out for me, and I appreciate that. I'll meet the right person in my own way when the time is right. For now, I'm taking a break from talking about dating." His answer role models an abundant, healthy attitude about dating, while also gently drawing boundaries. I next coached this guy to continue to wish his cousin well. Plus, to make a mental note to put his cousin in his outer circle of discussing dating. Protecting ourselves while having compassion for others is what *The Inner Circle/Outer Circle Plan* is all about!

Now it's your turn. Draw a circle inside a circle. In the outer circle ring, write the names of the people in your life who are emotionally fearful when it comes to dating. In the inner circle, write the names of your support system-people or creatures who uplift you in general and when it comes to discussing dating. Use *The Inner Circle/Outer Circle Plan* to protect yourself.

What and who would you put in your outer and inner circle?

YOUR TURN

Draw your *Inner Circle/Outer Circle Plan.*

CHERISH QUIET TIME, LISTEN TO YOUR INNER VOICE

I love quiet time, don't you? When you are single, you have the luxury of spending silent time alone. You learn to entertain yourself and you learn to feel your feelings. Whenever you are alone, cherish that time. Find that quiet inner voice that makes you feel calm. Using your quiet time to develop your selfhood enriches every area of your life!

All of us have a calm inner voice that makes us feel guided and grounded. Our inner voice says things to us like, "I'll meet the right person when the time is right." Our inner voice is our deepest, most loving self. We also have a voice of fear. This voice might say, "I'm not good enough." This voice is the side of us who feels wounded from childhood or judgment towards us.

We can train ourselves to heal the voice of fear by tapping into our loving inner voice. One woman told me, "I was disconnected from my guiding inner voice.

I kept hearing this critical voice, which was really the voice of one my parents. Over time I trained myself to call on the loving voice within me. Everything in life is better when you know how to be kind to yourself."

YOUR TURN

Call on your loving inner voice by saying: *What would love and wisdom say to me now?*

FINE TUNE YOUR IMAGE BY BECOMING A SMILER

"Whenever I see your smiling face, I have to smile myself." That James Taylor song is awesome. Plus, it's true! Smiling is one of the most powerful ways to draw people to you. When you make a habit of smiling in the morning, at work, in the mirror, when you walk down the street, your world opens up and you make everyone around you feel uplifted.

One past student emailed me, "I'm usually lost in thought and very serious as I go about my day. But one time, I received some great news at the office, and I smiled during my errands that afternoon. Three different guys said hello to me. One of them was walking behind me and as he passed by he said, 'Good morning!' The smile must have made me stand up straighter and given me a confident energy, even from behind. I felt like a new person. People treated me differently."

So how do you become a smiler? In the morning, before you leave home, make a list of what you love about your life. Focus on and think about all the positive aspects you have going for you. You will feel and look energized. One guy in class tried that technique and commented, "It works! Now I know how important is it to carry your blessings with you everywhere."

YOUR TURN

Write down your positive qualities. Remember past compliments. Write those down too. Now add to the list what you like about your life. Keep this list in your purse or wallet and read it every morning, before you go to sleep and whenever you need a self-esteem boost.

YOUR PASSION FOR LIFE INSPIRES OTHERS

Once I was sitting at Kinkos waiting for some copies. A guy walked in. He looked at me and said, "Do you have the PC 500 gigabyte storage system?" "Uh, I don't think so." I smiled. Then he became intensely animated and told me more. "That's the system I have! Yep. It's connected to my gigabyte transformer and I can't get the v-chips to download the cube chip..." He went on for awhile and even though I had no idea what he was talking about, I was taken with his passion. I just kept nodding and smiling and suddenly he jumped up, "That's it! I need to reboot the y-chip in a back-up hard drive. Thanks for solving my problem!" He shook my hand vigorously and ran out. I thought to myself, what an exciting guy!

Do you have something in your life that gives you joy and inspiration? Is it doing yoga? Fixing cars? Painting? Listening to music? Being in your garden? Cooking? Dancing? As you know, one of my passions is The Beatles. Sometimes I have my own personal Beatle-a-thons where I spend the entire weekend watching Beatle videos by myself. I also love going to concerts, reading pop-culture magazines, and I recently learned guitar and started studying Spanish. Find out what excites you and then explore the hobby of your choice. A hobby opens your world and guides you on the path of more discovery. Whether you are in a romantic relationship or not, having personal hobbies and interests is an important part of loving your life and helps you radiate an exciting energy to others!

YOUR TURN

Fill in the blanks: Some hobbies I've enjoyed in the past are_____. A new one I'm exploring is _____. One of my simple pleasures is _____.

Spending even minutes a day on a personal hobby makes you feel energized and creative. A hobby doesn't have to be intense either. It can be as simple as admiring flowers! I call one of my hobbies flirtography. I love to take pictures of people, nature and special moments in life. Once I develop the photos, I look for hidden pictures in each one. Remember my picture marching down Abbey Road? When I developed that, I saw a little face with dark glasses and a turned-up nose hidden in the bark of a tree. It looks like one of the early Beatle members, Stuart Sutcliffe, who passed away in his 20s. I see him in the tree cheering me on! In one of my cloud photos I see the image of an angel appearing in the sky! I like to share these photos in my seminars and see if people can spot hidden pictures, too. One guy said of my Abbey Road photo, "I don't see a face in the bark, but my grandfather is in that bush!" Flirtography is a blast!

Allow yourself the joy of finding things that you love to do. You will develop your own distinct style and when you meet the right person to date, you may have common interests. Plus, you'll continue to attract positive people into your life and you'll feel inspired everyday!

You've done amazing on these last bunch of flirtatious ideas! Here are some more.

CELEBRATE BEING SINGLE

"Life is peaceful...I can come and go as I please...I have the time and freedom to explore myself...I can walk in the house and throw my clothes on the floor!" When I ask students in my dating class what they like about being single, those are some of their answers.

There are a lot of benefits to being single, and appreciating those benefits makes you feel joyful, calm and draws positive people to you. Many people who rushed into marriage say they wish they had spent some time on their own, and they envy the freedom their single friends have. Happy singles comment on the confidence and independence they gain by spending time alone and having the luxury to focus on themselves.

One of the most exciting times of my single life was a trip I took to Israel alone. I was a little nervous, but I felt a sense of strength and power just making the journey. Traveling alone forced me to reach out to people and create opportunities for myself everywhere. I made friends with so many interesting people from all over the world. I felt a sense of magic! For example, I would wish for something simple like a bag of popcorn. The next thing you know, I stumbled by a store just as it was closing, and I spotted a popcorn machine, but I had no money. I said to the clerk, "Who gets the extra popcorn?" He smiled, handed me a bag and said, "You." Being grateful and appreciating your solitude opens up your life to more joy and magic.

YOUR TURN

Wherever you go, hold your head up high and be proud of your independence. Find new activities that you've always wanted to explore. Cherish your freedom and expect magic.

Reach out and ask questions. Be grateful for all the good things in your life.

FEEL GREAT AND DATE YOURSELF

Can you stay home alone on a Saturday night and have fun? When you enjoy your own company, you enter relationships for healthy reasons, to share yourself. When you don't like being with yourself, you often feel empty and look for someone to fill your needs. No one can do that until you fill your own needs. Being your own best friend is the first and most important step. By dating yourself you know what movies you like, what music you like to listen to, what kinds of books you like to read. If you can be a good date for yourself, you can be a good date with other people.

YOUR TURN

Pick a night to be alone and plan a date with yourself.

How would you spend your time?

What would you say to yourself?

If you feel you've had too many nights alone, ask yourself, have you been a good date to you? Were you conscious of giving yourself fun and thinking positive thoughts? If the answer is yes then you have conquered a major step in dating and feeling great!

STAY TRUE TO YOU

You don't have to get married. I tell you that because some people forget they have options. One woman in my dating class said, "I'm choosing to be single right now, and I'm happy. But sometimes I feel strange because my relatives ask me all the time, "When are we going to get you married?" This question can feel hurtful. It implies that who and where we are in our lives right now isn't enough. Don't take the question personally. People who ask us questions like that are projecting their expectations into our lives. Often these people never considered other ways to live and be happy. They just assume that everybody wants to get married and have children. Maybe they were never trained to listen to their heart or they would have made different choices.

One woman who called in my radio show said, "People in awful marriages always seem anxious for me to get married. Misery loves company, I guess."

Whatever the reason, it's so important to believe in
your own truth and don't let any other's expectations
affect you. There are so many different ways to live a
happy and fulfilling life! We owe it to ourselves to
choose the path that feels right to us.

I know a woman who has had the same boyfriend
for 30 years. She refers to him as her long-term
boyfriend. They love being boyfriend and girlfriend.
They live in separate houses, and they are not planning
on getting married. They like their relationship just the
way it is. Actors Goldie Hawn and Kurt Russell have
been living together for decades. They choose not to
marry, but they refer to each other as husband and wife
and say they feel married in their hearts. Their lifestyle
works for them and their children.

Live the lifestyle that feels right to you. What you
want in a relationship is out there waiting for you. You
are special regardless of your dating status!

YOUR TURN

Remind yourself: *I honor myself by choosing a path
that is right for me.*

THINK: *I AM A GREAT CATCH*

One dater wrote me with her results. "I hadn't been

on a date in two years, and I was feeling really discouraged. So I decided to repeat that slogan. I am a great catch. I'd repeat this to myself throughout the day and I began feeling much more confident. I even started sleeping better. After a month of repeating my slogan, a guy who lives in my building asked me out. At the end of the date he said to me, 'You are a great catch.' It was like he read my mind."

YOUR TURN

Every day tell yourself: *I am a great catch*!

THE SECRET TO SKYROCKETING YOUR CONFIDENCE: YOUR SUPER SLOGAN

Repeat after me, "It only takes one." One way to build your faith in your future is to invent your own slogan, something you can repeat to yourself that makes you feel calm, hopeful and confident. That slogan, "It only takes one," has helped a lot of people. I had a sweet, fun-loving friend in high school who never dated, not once. I'm sure she would have liked to have had a date or a boyfriend, but she kept herself optimistic by reminding herself that "It only takes one." She went on to college, where she didn't date anyone and after college she moved to Colorado for a new job. At that job she met a great guy. They eventually married and had children. She was right. It only takes one and she found him. One woman in class told me that slogan helps her stay alert and notice people wherever she goes. She used to get lost in her own thoughts, but now she looks around and thinks, "I wonder if the one is around here?"

One of my personal slogans is "Honor the turtle," which I tell myself when I need patience. I look at patience as the willpower to trust life's process, and I wished for the perfect slogan to remind me of that. A turtle inspired my slogan! One day Joe and I were crossing the street as we walked to the lake. We noticed a turtle on the ground who had moss all over his shell. He was ever so slowly crawling across the street. We picked him up, held him out in front of us and walked him to the lake. He stuck his head and arms out like when Superman flies! Then we reached the lake and put him in the water. He did a giant turtle breast stroke and the moss flew off his back! I remember feeling so inspired by that moment. The turtle showed me that if I'm patient, positive and take my time, life will bring me just where I need to be.

YOUR TURN

If you ever need patience, remember the slogan: *It only takes one* **or** *I trust life's process* **or** *Honor the turtle.* **Take a second right now and create** *Your Super Slogan.*

PACE YOURSELF

Does making the effort to date ever feel like a job? One woman told me, "Every Friday and Saturday night I get all dressed up and either attend a singles event or go on a blind date or go to the bars to check out the guys. I know it should be fun, but I'm exhausted. The effort is tiring." When making an effort to date or meet someone feels exhausting, it's time to take a break. Give yourself a few weeks off. Put your dating efforts aside and try not to even to think about it. By taking time off you get back into yourself and you recharge your own emotional battery.

One tired dater told me, "I was burned out from trying to date and yet I was obsessed with it, too. I finally marked off a month on my calendar. Every time I was tempted to think about dating, I'd look at my calendar and think, oh yeah, I'm on vacation. I really learned to let go that month, and I learned to like my life even more."

Everything in life goes in cycles just like the seasons in nature. There will be times you'll like the idea of making an effort in the dating arena and there will be times you'll want to put dating out of your mind. Respect your feelings and work with the cycles. Life has a special way of working everything out.

YOUR TURN

When the idea of dating or making an effort to date feels draining, take an official break.

Mark the time off on your calendar and celebrate all the other areas in your life. You'll feel energized to think about dating later and romance may find you in the meantime.

BEFORE YOU FIND "THE ONE," BE "THE ONE"

"Jill, let me give you some true confessions of a groupie," one woman I coached told me. She said, "I used to follow rock groups around and try to meet the lead singers. I would obsess about them! Then I realized the reason I chased rock stars was because I wanted to be like them. They are so artistic and confident. So I decided to focus on my own artistic interests. Now I'm singing for a startup band and singing in choir at Church. I feel good about myself. Even though I still love music I don't feel the need to chase rock stars. I feel fulfilled from within." Sometimes when we are looking for someone with special qualities, we also seek those qualities in ourselves.

Be the type of person you want to be with. Are you seeking someone who is passionate about life and self-assured? Develop those qualities in yourself first. That way you live a meaningful life and attract similar people into your life.

YOUR TURN

When you think of "the one," what are you looking for?

Are you developing those qualities in yourself?

I know you are!

SUMMARY PEP TALK

You are almost done! We are down to the last pages!
Let's take a quick review of this last chapter.

*Always look at dating as a spiritual journey.
Remember everything happens for a reason and at the
right time. Look for people who validate your journey
and include positive, encouraging people in your inner
circle.

*Cherish the quiet time you have in your life. Train
yourself to listen to your loving, guiding voice within.
Celebrate the fact that you are single. Now is the time
to embrace your freedom and explore your hobbies and
interests.

*Fine tune your inner and outer image by becoming
a smiler. Count your blessings in your mind. Repeat to
yourself *I am a great catch!* Develop other inspira-
tional slogans for yourself, such as *It only takes one* or
Honor the turtle.

YOU ARE A GREAT CATCH!

START CELEBRATING RIGHT NOW

Congratulations! You are almost done reading this book.

You should be proud of yourself. Reading this book is taking a giant step towards yourself. When you're committed to your own growth and happiness, life rushes towards you!

As soon as you finish this book I want you to give yourself a round of applause. If you don't want to do it out loud, applaud yourself in your mind. Practice being proud of yourself on a daily basis. The more you appreciate your own strength and power, the stronger you become. You are a great catch. You are a special person. Here's to you!

YOUR TURN

Take a few moments and praise yourself for being committed to your growth.

APPRECIATE THE MAGIC IN YOUR LIFE

The most important part of having a great romance in your life is having a romance with life! Look for the synchronicity and coincidences that happen to you every day. Did you run into someone you were just thinking about? Were you wishing for a certain item and then somebody just handed it to you? Were you remembering a movie you loved and then it played on television that night? By paying attention to all the little pieces of magic that happen to you, you'll have an energizing, flirtatious connection with life and you'll build faith in your future.

Take time to celebrate the simple pleasures that give you joy, like the soothing feel of a warm day, the satisfaction of giving a compliment, the charge your favorite song gives you, the relaxation of taking a weekend nap, the excitement of reading an awesome book, the smile that comes over you when you see a puppy. Cherish all of life's magic! Appreciating each moment makes life so rich and full. The joy you seek in dating is already inside you and all around you!

Expect to date and feel great.

The best is yet to come!

WRITE ME AND TELL ME YOUR STORY

I'm thrilled that you read this book. I want to hear your thoughts and what happens to you. My email address is Jill@Flirtnow.com. I'm wishing you happiness and success, and I know you are drawing it to you right now!